Founders

Founders

Alan S. Gutterman

BEP BUSINESS EXPERT PRESS

Founders

First published in 2018 by
Business Expert Press, LLC
222 East 46th Street, New York, NY 10017
www.businessexpertpress.com

ISBN-13: 978-1-94897-655-8 (paperback)
ISBN-13: 978-1-94897-656-5 (e-book)

Business Expert Press Entrepreneurship and Small Business Management Collection

Collection ISSN: 1946-5653 (print)
Collection ISSN: 1946-5661 (electronic)

Cover and interior design by Exeter Premedia Services Private Ltd., Chennai, India

First edition: 2018

10 9 8 7 6 5 4 3 2 1

Printed in the United States of America.

Abstract

The terms "founder" and "promoter" are used frequently when discussing new businesses. Neither of these terms has a particular technical legal meaning and they are used somewhat interchangeably in practice. However, it is useful and accurate to think of a "founder" as a person who assists in the formation of a new business and then continues to devote a significant amount of time and resources to the operation of business once it has been formed. The founders often become the officers, directors, general partners, or managing members, and the term "founding shareholder" or "founding president," for example, is often used to refer to one of the first shareholders of a corporation or a corporation's first president. A promoter, on the other hand, is a person, including possibly a legal entity, who assists in the formation of a business entity or obtaining subscriptions for its ownership interests, but who does not necessarily have any continuing relationship to the business once it is formed and funded. It is not surprising to find that founders play a pivotal role in the success of any new business even in situations where the founder is active in the business for only a short period of time and responsibility for oversight of the business is turned over to professional managers who were not affiliated with the business at inception. Founders not only bring the original business idea to the table, but they also have a substantial influence on the organizational culture and values and goals of the initial managers and employees who live on for a significant period of time. This book covers a variety of topics relating to founders, beginning with an overview of the motivational traits of prospective entrepreneurs and the role that entrepreneurs play in launching new businesses and then moving on the personality traits and skill sets of those persons who seek to form new business followed by a discussion of some of the practical issues relating to founders with respect to their preformation duties and liabilities, particularly their relationships with prior employers, and their relationships and agreements with other members of the founding group. The book also examines the role that founders have on the organizational culture of their firms and the positions that founders occupy if and when their firms reach the point where they are ready to take on the rigors of public company status and complete an initial public offering of their securities. This book is a "must have" guide for anyone thinking about launching a new business and also is an excellent resource for attorneys and other professionals providing advice to their clients and academics teaching entrepreneurship classes.

Keywords

entrepreneurship, founders, founder's relationships, launching a business, organizational culture

Contents

CHAPTER 1

Motivational Traits of Prospective Entrepreneurs

Introduction

Gartner described the "trait approach" to studying entrepreneurship as based on the assumption that "the entrepreneur is . . . a particular personality type, a fixed state of existence, a desirable species that one might find a picture of in a field guide" and explained that research based on this approach has necessarily focused on identifying and enumerating a set of characteristics (i.e., traits) that describe this idealized type of person we call an "entrepreneur."[1] Gartner described the activities of researchers quite simply asking the question: "Who is an entrepreneur?" This approach assumes that a person, the "entrepreneur," is the basic unit of analysis when it comes to studying the launch of a new business and that in order to understand new business creation it is necessary to analyze the characteristics and traits of the entrepreneur and how they "cause" the new business to emerge. Research based on the trait approach has been voluminous and has dominated much of the early activities within entrepreneurship research. A comprehensive list of characteristics that researchers have attempted to relate to entrepreneurship would include risk-taking propensity; educational background of the entrepreneur and his or her parents; number of previous jobs and previous job satisfaction; social attitudes; religious, sports, and club affiliations; age; need for achievement; desire for autonomy and independence; level of aggression; locus of control; perception of opportunities offered by society; self-discipline and perseverance; energy level; self-reliance; desire for success

---

[1] Gartner, W.B. Spring 1988. "'Who Is an Entrepreneur?' Is the Wrong Question." *American Journal of Small Business* 12, no. 4, pp. 11–32.

and recognition; tolerance of uncertainty; creativity; support; benevolence; optimism; self-esteem and Machiavellianism.[2]

Motivational Traits and Their Effect on Entrepreneurship

Shane et al. argued strongly that differences among people with respect to their personal motivations significantly influenced their actions during the entrepreneurial process and that it was incumbent upon researchers to incorporate individual-level variations in motivations into the study of entrepreneurship.[3] They noted, for example, that people differ in their perceptions of risk[4] and that these differences may lead two people confronted with a similar opportunity to come to different conclusions about whether they are willing to expend their resources on the opportunity before having a better idea of the distribution of possible outcomes from the investment. Similarly, persons who score higher on measures of optimism or self-efficacy may be more willing than persons with lower scores on those personal characteristics to take on pursuit of an opportunity that carries a fairly low likelihood of success.

Shane et al. provided a concise summary of some of the quantitative and qualitative research relating to human motivations and their effect on entrepreneurship. They focused on previous research that had explored human motivations and their effect on entrepreneurship and divided the work into quantitative and qualitative studies. Many of the quantitative studies compared the traits of "firm founders" (i.e., persons who start

---

[2] Id. at pp. 13–20. "Founder's Traits and Skills." in *Entrepreneurship: A Library of Resources for Sustainable Entrepreneurs.* prepared and distributed by the Sustainable Entrepreneurship Project (www.seproject.org) includes additional discussion of the personality traits of persons likely to start a new business and the personal and professional skills that founders should possess in order to increase their likelihood of success in launching a new business.

[3] Shane. S., E. Locke, and C. Collins. 2003. "Entrepreneurial Motivation." *Human Resource Management Review* 13, no. 2, pp. 257–79, 260.

[4] See, for example, Palich. L., and D. Bagby. 1995. "Using Cognitive Theory to Explain Entrepreneurial Risk-Taking: Challenging Conventional Wisdom." *Journal of Business Venturing* 10, no. 6, pp. 425–38.

their own business), typically assumed to be the "entrepreneurs," to other persons in the general population and also compared the traits of firm founders to persons who acted in a managerial capacity in businesses owned by others. Shane et al. acknowledged that the comparison of firm founders and managers who worked for others as a means of capturing differences between entrepreneurial and nonentrepreneurial situations might not be completely appropriate since "serving as a manager in a rapidly growing high-technology company might demand greater entrepreneurial motivations than starting a corner grocery store."[5] Common motivational traits explored in the quantitative studies included need for achievement, risk-taking, tolerance for ambiguity, locus of control, self-efficacy, and goal setting. Motivational traits explored in the qualitative studies included independence, competence and confidence, drive and egoistic passion.[6]

Shane et al. cautioned that their work did not constitute a complete review of prior empirical research due to the fact that the definitions of entrepreneurship used in previous studies were inconsistent with the definition used by Shane et al., making it impossible to draw direct implications of prior work for research using their definition, and their belief that prior research suffered from "significant methodological problems," which are discussed below.[7] Shane et al. noted that many researchers

---

[5] Shane, S., E. Locke, and C. Collins. 2003. "Entrepreneurial Motivation." *Human Resource Management Review* 13, no. 2, pp. 257–79, 267.

[6] The analysis included observations from an inductive study based on secondary sources of 70 wealth creators completed by Locke. Locke explored the careers, actions, and traits of legendary businesspersons such as J.P. Morgan, Steve Jobs, Sam Walton, Walt Disney, Jack Welch, Thomas Edison, Michael Dell, Henry Ford, and Ray Kroc and identified several common characteristics such as independent vision, an active mind, competence and confidence, drive to action, egotistic passion and love of ability in others. See Locke, E. 2000. *The Prime Movers: Traits of the Great Wealth Creators*. New York, NY: AMACOM.

[7] Shane, S., E. Locke, and C. Collins. 2003. "Entrepreneurial Motivation." *Human Resource Management Review* 13, no. 2, pp. 257–79, 263. For example., other traits that researchers have focused on to differentiate entrepreneurs from non-entrepreneurs have included "values" (see, e.g., DeCarlo, J., and P. Lyons. 1979. "A Comparison of Selected Personal Characteristics of Minor-

had expressed "disappointment" with the results of the prior research; however, they claimed that their discussion was useful and necessary in illustrating how personal motivation can influence different aspects of the entrepreneurial process and, as discussed below, offered their own suggestions for how entrepreneurial motivation might be incorporated into the study and understanding of the entrepreneurial process.[8]

Need for Achievement

A high "need for achievement," a concept made famous by McClelland, is often cited as a predictor of the likelihood that a person will be interested in pursuing entrepreneurial activities rather than other types of jobs. Not surprisingly, need for achievement (nAch) has been frequently studied by researchers interested in entrepreneurship. At the outset, McClelland postulated that "individuals who are high in nAch are more likely than those who are low in nAch to engage in activities or tasks that have a high degree of individual responsibility for outcomes, require individual skill and effort, have a moderate degree of risk, and include clear feedback on

---

ity and Non-Minority Female Entrepreneurs." *Journal of Small Business Management* 17, pp. 22–29); Hornaday, J., and J. Aboud. 1971. "Characteristics of Successful Entrepreneurs." *Personnel Psychology* 24, no. 2, pp. 141–53; Hull, D., J. Bosley, and G. Udell. 1980. "Reviewing the Heffalump: Identifying Potential Entrepreneurs by Personality Characteristics." *Journal of Small Business Management* 18, pp. 11–18; Komives, J. 1972. "A Preliminary Study of the Personal Values of High Technology Entrepreneurs." In *Technical Entrepreneurship: A Symposium Milwaukee, WI: Center for Venture Management*, eds. A. Cooper and J. Komives, 231-42 and "age" (see, e.g., Cooper, A., and W. Dunkelberg. 1981. "A New Look at Business Entry: Experiences of 1805 Entrepreneurs." In *Frontiers of Entrepreneurship Research: The Proceedings of the Babson Conference on Entrepreneurship Research*, ed. K. Vesper, 1–20. Wellesley, MA: Babson College). Howell, R. 1972. "Comparative Profiles: Entrepreneurs Versus The Hired Executives: San Francisco Peninsula Semiconductor Industry." In *Technical entrepreneurship: A Symposium*, eds. A. Cooper and J. Komives, 47–62. Milwaukee, WI: Center for Venture Management.

[8] Shane, S., E. Locke, and C. Collins. 2003. "Entrepreneurial Motivation." *Human Resource Management Review* 13, no. 2, pp. 257–79.

performance."[9] McClelland also believed that entrepreneurial roles have more of the aforementioned activity or task attributes than other roles, thus leading to the conclusion that high achievers will likely gravitate toward entrepreneurship. In general, studies have confirmed the apparent relationship between nAch and entrepreneurship.[10] In addition, nAch has been found to be a differentiator between firm founders from members of the general population and to be useful in differentiating between successful and unsuccessful firm founders; however, there appears to be little difference between firm founders and managers with respect to their levels of nAch.[11]

Risk Taking

Not surprisingly, it has often been argued that persons with an entrepreneurial bent of mind have a higher tolerance for accepting risk and uncertainty.[12] As noted above, one of the characteristics of high nAch

---

[9] Id. citing McClelland, D. 1961. *The Achieving Society.* Princeton, NJ: Van Nostrand.

[10] See, for example, Johnson, B. 1990. "Toward a Multidimensional Model of Entrepreneurship: The Case of Achievement Motivation and the Entrepreneur." *Entrepreneurship Theory and Practice* 14, no. 3, pp. 39–54; Komives, J. 1972. "A Preliminary Study of the Personal Values of High Technology Entrepreneurs." In *Technical Entrepreneurship: A Symposium*, eds. A. Cooper and J. Komives, 231–42. Milwaukee, WI: Center for Venture Management; and McClelland, D., and D. Winter. 1969. *Motivating Economic Achievement.* New York, NY: Free Press.

[11] Shane, S., E. Locke, and C. Collins. 2003. "Entrepreneurial Motivation." *Human Resource Management Review* 13, no. 2, pp. 257–79, 264 (citing Collins, C., E. Locke, and P. Hanges. 2000. "The Relationship of Need for Achievement to Entrepreneurial Behavior: A Meta-Analysis." Working paper, University of Maryland, College Park, MD).

[12] Venkataraman. S. 1997. "The Distinctive Domain of Entrepreneurship Research: An Editor's Perspective." In *Advances in Entrepreneurship, Firm Emergence and Growth*, eds. J. Katz and R. Brockhaus, 119–38. 3 vols. Greenwich, CT: JAI Press (noting that several theories of entrepreneurship view entrepreneurs as willing to bear residual uncertainty). See also Brockhaus, R. 1980. "Risk Taking Propensity of Entrepreneurs." *Academy of Management Journal* 23, no. 3, pp. 509–20; Hull, D., J. Bosley, and G. Udell. 1980. "Reviewing the

cited by McClelland is a willingness and desire to engage in activities with a "moderate degree of risk" and Liles argued that entrepreneurs understand that they will be required to live with uncertainty with respect to financial and psychic well-being, career security, and relations with their family members.[13] There appears to be general agreement that extremely high levels of risk are not necessary in order for an activity to qualify as "entrepreneurial." According to Shane et al., "risk-taking propensity has been defined in the entrepreneurship literature as the willingness to take moderate risks."[14] Interestingly, however, the feedback from studies on this issue is mixed and many researchers have failed to find significant differences between firm owners and the general population with respect to risk-taking propensity and studies that did find a difference between those two groups failed to find significant differences between firm founders and managers.[15] Shane et al. suggest that the reason for these findings may be explained by "self-efficacy" and point to several evaluative studies based

---

Heffalump: Identifying Potential Entrepreneurs by Personality Characteristics." *Journal of Small Business Management* 18, pp. 11–18; and Palmer, M. 1971. "The Application of Psychological Testing to Entrepreneurial Potential." *California Management Review* 13, no. 3, pp. 32–39.

[13] Liles, P. 1974. *New Business Ventures and the Entrepreneur Homewood.* IL: Irwin; and Liles, P. 1974. "Who are the Entrepreneurs?" *MSU Business Topics* 22, pp. 5–14.

[14] Shane, S., E. Locke, and C. Collins. 2003. "Entrepreneurial Motivation." *Human Resource Management Review* 13, no. 2, pp. 257–79, 265 (citing Begley, T. 1995. "Using Founder Status, Age of Firm and Company Growth Rate as the basis for Distinguishing Entrepreneurs from Managers of Small Businesses." *Journal of Business Venturing* 10, no. 3, pp. 249–63.)

[15] Id. citing Kogan, N., and M. Wallach. 1964. *Risk Taking.* New York, NY: Holt, Rinehart and Winston; Litzinger, W. 1961. "The Motel Entrepreneur and the Motel Manager." *Academy of Management Journal* 8, no. 4, pp. 268–81; and Low, M.B., and I.C. MacMillan. 1988. "Entrepreneurship: Past Research and Future Challenges." *Journal of Management* 14, no. 2, pp. 139–61. However, in a study conducted by Bagley on the differences among New England business executives, risk-taking propensity was the only trait on which founders and non-founders differed. See Begley, T. 1995. "Using Founder Status, Age of Firm and Company Growth Rate as the Basis for Distinguishing Entrepreneurs from Managers of Small Businesses." *Journal of Business Venturing* 10, no. 3, pp. 249–63.

on interviews and expert evaluations that concluded that firm founders did indeed have a higher propensity for risk than the general population on objective scales of measurement yet often did not perceive their actions to be risky.[16] Another study comparing firm founders to bankers found that while the bankers perceived information regarding certain opportunities as risky the firm founders were more interested in the opportunities associated with the information.[17]

Tolerance for Ambiguity

The tolerance for ambiguity, which has been described as "the propensity to view situations without clear outcomes as attractive rather than threatening,"[18] has been cited as an important trait for entrepreneurs given that starting and building a new business requires overcoming challenges that are unpredictable and it is extremely difficult to measure the chances for success.[19] While this sounds reasonable, actual studies on this proposition have produced mixed results. On the one hand, several researchers have found that founders have a significantly higher tolerance for ambiguity than managers.[20] However, others were unable to replicate that result and

---

[16] Id. citing Corman, J., B. Perles, and P. Vancini. 1988. "Motivational Factors Influencing High-Technology Entrepreneurship." *Journal of Small Business Management* 26, no. 1, pp. 36–42; and Fry, F. 1993. *Entrepreneurship: A Planning Approach.* Minneapolis-St. Paul, MN: West Publishing.

[17] Sarasvathy, D., H. Simon, and L. Lave. 1998. "Perceiving and Managing Business Risks: Differences Between Entrepreneurs and Bankers." *Journal of Economic Behavior and Organization* 33, no. 2, pp. 207–25.

[18] Stanley Budner, N.Y. 1962. "Intolerance of Ambiguity as a Personality Variable." *Journal of Personality* 30, no. 1, pp. 29–50.

[19] Schere, J. 1992. "Tolerance of Ambiguity as a Discriminating Variable Between Entrepreneurs and Managers." *Academy of Management Best Paper Proceedings* 42, pp. 404–08.

[20] Begley, T., and D. Boyd. 1987. "A comparison of Entrepreneurs and Managers of Small Business Firms." *Journal of Management* 13, no. 1, pp. 99–108; Miller, D., and C. Drodge. 1986. "Psychological and Traditional Determinants of Structure." *Administrative Science Quarterly* 31, pp. 539–60; Sexton, D., and N. Bowman. 1986. "Validation of a Personality Index: Comparative Psychological Characteristics Analysis of Female Entrepreneurs, Managers, Entrepreneurship

found no significant differences between founders and managers with respect to their tolerance for ambiguity.[21]

Locus of Control

Locus of control refers to "the belief in the extent to which individuals believe that their actions or personal characteristics affect outcomes."[22] Distinctions are made between persons who have an "external" locus of control and thus believe that outcomes are generally determined by factors outside of their control and persons with an "internal" locus of control who believe that they can have an impact on outcomes through the choices they make with regard to their personal actions. Persons with high nAch generally have a preference for situations in which they can have direct control over outcomes and researchers have predicted that persons with an internal locus of control are more likely to seek out entrepreneurial roles in which their actions have a stronger influence on the results of their entrepreneurial activities.[23] In general, research confirms that firm founders are more "internal" than the general public with regard to locus of control[24]; however, as is the case with nAch, comparisons

---

Students, and Business Students." *In Frontiers of Entrepreneurship Research*, 513–28. Wellesley, MA: Babson College.

[21] Babb, E.M., and S.V. Babb. 1992. "Psychological Traits of Rural Entrepreneurs." *Journal of Socio-Economics* 21, no. 4, pp. 353–62; and Begley, T. 1995. "Using Founder Status, Age of Firm, and Company Growth Rate as the Basis for Distinguishing Entrepreneurs form Managers of Smaller Businesses." *Journal of Business Venturing* 10, no. 3, pp. 249–63.

[22] Shane, S., E. Locke, and C. Collins. 2003. "Entrepreneurial Motivation." *Human Resource Management Review* 13, no. 2, pp. 257–79, 266.

[23] Rotter, J. 1966. "Generalized Expectancies for Internal Versus External Control of Reinforcement." *Psychological Monographs: General and Applied* 80, no. 1, p. 609.

[24] See, for example, Bowen, D., and R. Hisrich. 1986. "The Female Entrepreneur: A Career Development Perspective." *Academy of Management Review* 11, no. 2, pp. 393–407; Durand, D. 1975. "Effects of Achievement Motivation and Skill Training on the Entrepreneurial Behavior of Black Businessmen." *Organizational Behavior and Human Performance* 14, no. 1, pp. 76–90; and Shapero, A. 1977. "The Displaced, Uncomfortable Entrepreneur." *Psychology Today* 9, pp. 83–88.

of firm founders and managers usually find no significant differences between them with regard to locus of control.[25]

Self-Efficacy

Bandura described "self-efficacy" as one's belief in his or her own ability to muster and implement the necessary personal resources, skills, and competencies that are required in order to attain a certain level of achievement on a given task.[26] Simply put, individuals who are high on self-efficacy are more "self-confident" with respect to the particular task and, in fact, Shane et al. reported that "[s]elf-efficacy for a specific task has been shown to be a robust predictor of an individual's performance in that task and helps to explain why people of equal ability can perform differently."[27]

---

[25] See, for example, Babb, E., and S. Babb. 1992. "Psychological Traits of Rural Entrepreneurs." *Journal of Socio-Economics* 21, no. 4, pp. 353–62; Brockhaus, R. 1982. "The Psychology of the Entrepreneur." In *Encyclopedia of Entrepreneurship*, eds. C. Kent, D. Sexton and K. Vesper, 39–57. Englewood Cliffs, NJ: Prentice-Hall; Hull, D., J. Bosley, and G. Udell. 1980. "Renewing the Hunt for Heffalump: Identifying Potential Entrepreneurs by Personality Characteristics." *Journal of Small Business* 18, pp. 11–18; Begley, T. 1995. "Using Founder Status, Age of Firm, and Company Growth Rate as the Basis for Distinguishing Entrepreneurs from Managers of Smaller Businesses." *Journal of Business Venturing* 10, no. 3, pp. 249–63; Begley, T., and D. Boyd. 1987. "A Comparison of Entrepreneurs and Managers of Small Business Firms." *Journal of Management* 13, no. 1, pp. 99–108; Brockhaus, R. 1980. "Risk Taking Propensity of Entrepreneurs." *Academy of Management Journal* 23, no. 3, pp. 509–20; Brockhaus, R., and W. Nord. 1979. "An Exploration of Factors Affecting the Entrepreneurial Decision: Personal Characteristics VS Environmental Conditions." *Proceedings of the Annual Meeting of the Academy of Management*; and Liles, P. 1974. "Who are the Entrepreneurs?" *MSU Business Topics* 22, pp. 5–14. For further discussion of the literature relating to entrepreneurship and "internal locus of control," see also Mueller, S., and A. Thomas. 2000. "Culture and Entrepreneurial Potential: A Nine Country Study of Locus of Control and Innovativeness." *Journal of Business Venturing* 16, nos. 51–75, pp. 55–57. (including extensive citations).

[26] Bandura, A. 1997. *Self-Efficacy: The Exercise of Self Control.* New York, NY: Freeman.

[27] Shane, S., E. Locke, and C. Collins. 2003. "Entrepreneurial Motivation." *Human Resource Management Review* 13, no. 2, pp. 257–79, 267.

One study of entrepreneurs found that there was a strong and positive relationship between self-efficacy to grow a company and the growth actually realized by the company.[28] The presence of self-efficacy explains why persons are willing to exert longer and harder effort on completion of a given task; persist in the face of setbacks; set higher goals with respect to financial performance, growth, and innovation; and develop and refine better plans and strategies to achieve their goals.[29]

Independence

Shane et al. described independence as "taking responsibility to use one's own judgment as opposed to blinding following the assertions of others . . . [and] . . . taking responsibility for one's own life rather than living off the efforts of others."[30] A number of studies have uncovered evidence to support the widely held belief that entrepreneurship requires independence and that entrepreneurs score higher on measures of independence than members of the general public.[31] Entrepreneurship is an attractive

---

[28] Id. (citing Baum, R. 1994. "The Relation of Traits, Competencies, Vision, Motivation, and Strategy to Venture Growth." *Unpublished Doctoral Dissertation.* University of Maryland, College Park, MD). See also Chandler, G., and E. Jansen. 1992. "The Founder's Self-Assessed Competence and Venture Performance." *Journal of Business Venturing 7*, no. 3, pp. 223–36.

[29] Several studies have confirmed the importance of "goal setting" by reporting that the goals established by entrepreneurs with respect to financial performance, growth, and innovation were significantly related to the corresponding outcomes. Id. at p. 267 citing Tracy, K., E. Locke, and M. Renard. 1998. "Conscious Goal Setting Versus Subconscious Motives: Longitudinal and Concurrent Effects on the Performance of Entrepreneurial Firms." Paper Presented at the meeting of the Academy of Management, Boston, MA; and Baum, J., E. Locke, and K. Smith. 2001. "A Multi-Dimensional Model of Venture Growth." *Academy of Management Journal 44*, no. 2, pp. 292–303.

[30] Id. at p. 268.

[31] See, for example, Hisrich, R. 1985. "The Woman Entrepreneur in the United States and Puerto Rico: A Comparative Study." *Leadership and Organizational Development Journal 5*, no. 5, pp. 3–8; and Hornaday, J., and J. Aboud. 1971. "Characteristics of Successful Entrepreneurs." *Personnel Psychology 24*, no. 2, pp. 141–53.

alternative for persons who seek independence in their careers and work activities and provide persons with the opportunity to set their own goals and be responsible for results, regardless of whether they are successful or not.

Drive

Drive is related to nAch; however, Shane et al. used the term to focus specifically on "the willingness to put forth effort—both the effort of thinking and the effort involved in bringing one's ideas into reality."[32] Shane et al. argued that there were four aspects of "drive," including ambition, goals, energy, and stamina. Ambition is particularly important since it influences the desire of entrepreneurs to achieve "great, important and significant" things when pursuing their entrepreneurial activities. Ambition also causes entrepreneurs to set challenging goals, and research has confirmed that creating high goals leads to performance that is better than when the goals are more modest.[33] Other terms used to describe "drive" include "persistence" and "tenacity." Persons with high self-efficacy are more likely to have the drive necessary for the lengthy periods of hard work necessary for successful entrepreneurship.

Egoistic Passion

Shane et al. referred to "egoistic passion" as "a passionate, selfish love of work" that is largely ego-driven: the entrepreneur is driven by his or her "love [of] the process of building an organization and making it profitable."[34] Apparently, passion has often been included in studies of motivations among entrepreneurs; however, one study conducted by

---

[32] Shane, S., E. Locke, and C. Collins. 2003. "Entrepreneurial Motivation." *Human Resource Management Review* 13, no. 2, pp. 257–79, 268.

[33] Locke, E., and G. Latham. 1990. *A Theory of Goal Setting and Performance.* Englewood Cliffs, NJ: Prentice-Hall.

[34] Shane, S., E. Locke, and C. Collins. 2003. "Entrepreneurial Motivation." *Human Resource Management Review.* 13, no. 2, pp. 257–79, 268, 270–72.

Baum et al. did uncover evidence that passion had a direct and significant impact on the growth of firms.[35]

Critiques of Prior Research and Suggestions for Improvement

After presenting the results of their survey Shane et al. observed that the various studies had often come up with "disappointing results"[36] and Gartner also reported that the empirical research of others led them to conclude "that when certain psychological traits are carefully evaluated, it is not possible to differentiate entrepreneurs from managers or from the general population based on the entrepreneur's supposed possession of such traits."[37] Shane went on to identify several problems with previous research on human motivation and entrepreneurship.[38] One of the biggest concerns expressed by Shane et al. was the failure of prior researchers to

---

[35] Baum, J., E. Locke, and K. Smith. 2001. "A Multi-Dimensional Model of Venture Growth." *Academy of Management Journal* 44, no. 2, pp. 292–303.

[36] Shane, S., E. Locke, and C. Collins. 2003. "Entrepreneurial Motivation." *Human Resource Management Review* 13, no. 2, pp. 257–79, 269. (citing Busenitz, L., and J. Barney. 1997. "Differences Between Entrepreneurs and Managers in Large Organizations: Biases and Heuristics in Strategic Decision Making." *Journal of Business Venturing* 12, no. 1, pp. 9–30).

[37] Gartner, W. 1988. "'Who Is an Entrepreneur?' Is the Wrong Question." *American Journal of Small Business* 12, no. 4, pp. 11–32. (citing Brockhaus, R. 1980. "Risk Taking Propensity of Entrepreneurs." *Academy of Management Journal* 23, no. 3, pp. 509–20); Brockhaus. R., and W. Nord. 1979. "An Exploration of Factors Affecting the Entrepreneurial Decision: Personal Characteristics VS. Environmental Conditions." *Proceedings of the Annual Meeting of the Academy of Management*; and Sexton, D., and C. Kent. 1981. "Female Executives Versus Female Entrepreneurs." In *Frontiers of Entrepreneurship Research: The Proceeding of the 1981 Babson Conference on Entrepreneurship Research*, ed. K. Vesper, 40–45. Wellesley, MA: Babson College.

[38] Shane, S., E. Locke, and C. Collins. 2003. "Entrepreneurial Motivation." *Human Resource Management Review* 13, no. 2, pp. 257–79, 269–74. For more critiques of research on the role of human motivation in entrepreneurship, see Aldrich, H., and C. Zimmer. 1986. "Entrepreneurship through Social Networks." In *The Art and Science of Entrepreneurship*, eds. D. Sexton and R. Smilor, 3–23. Cambridge, MA: Ballinger; and Carroll, G., and E. Mosakowski. 1987.

recognize that entrepreneurship should be viewed as a "process" and that the influence of particular factors, such as one of the motivational traits, may vary depending upon where one is in the continuum of the process and the decisions that must be made and the actions that must be taken at that point. In fact, Shane et al. felt that one of the major shortcomings with the prior research on entrepreneurship had been that entrepreneurship was viewed as a profession that persons either chose or rejected and they commented that "relatively little of the motivation research on entrepreneurship has considered the effects of motivation on specific steps in the entrepreneurial process."[39]

Shane et al. also felt that the standard approach of comparing firm founders to one another, managers, and/or the general public at a single point in time was problematic since the assumptions were that a given motivation was equally relevant to each step in the entrepreneurial process and that the pool of persons in the "entrepreneurial group" remained that same throughout the process. They pointed out, for example, that a high level of self-confidence may be the most important motivational factor for "collection and assembly of resources," one of the tasks that must be completed at the execution stage of the entrepreneurial process described elsewhere in this chapter, and that the presence or absence of other motivational factors at that point is relatively unimportant. If this was true, it might explain why a firm founder who was high on all of the surveyed motivational factors other than self-confidence might nonetheless fail in his or her pursuit of a particular opportunity.[40] Shane et al. also went on to argue that if high self-confidence was the key motivator at the resource collection stage then those firm founders with low self-confidence were probably eliminated at that point (i.e., their ventures failed due to lack of resources) and confidence ceased to be a significant distinguishing factor among the firm founders who survived to reach the next stages in the process since they all had to have scored high on self-confidence to overcome

---

"The Career Dynamics of Self-Employment." *Administrative Science Quarterly* 32, pp. 570–89.

[39] Shane, S., E. Locke, and C. Collins. 2003. "Entrepreneurial Motivation." *Human Resource Management Review* 13, no. 2, pp. 257–79, 271.

[40] Id.

the resource collection hurdle. In the same vein, they pointed out that a high score on one of the motivating factors did not necessarily guarantee success of the venture or the activity if that factor was only relevant to one of the steps in entrepreneurial process. For example, high nAch may be quite important in impressing venture capitalists to provide capital for the business; however, once the money is in nAch may have little or no effect on completion of the subsequent steps in the process that will determine whether or not the firm is successful.

Other problems cited by Shane et al. included failure to control for variations in the opportunities available to prospective entrepreneurs, studying the "wrong motives," failure to consider the indirect effects of motives on other factors such as cognitive skills, strategy, and environmental conditions, and inconsistent definitions of "entrepreneurship." However, in spite of all the shortcomings and inadequacies in prior research work relating to human motivations in the entrepreneurial process, Shane et al. argued that the role that motivations play with respect to entrepreneurship should not be minimized and that the better approach was to develop and test a new model of how the motivational traits of prospective entrepreneurs combined with other factors to influence the entrepreneurial process. This model is the basis of the discussion of multifactor analysis of entrepreneurial activity that follows below.

Not surprisingly, Shane is not alone in criticizing the manner in which research on entrepreneurship has been conducted and the failure of researchers to look beyond a search for entrepreneurial traits or characteristics. Gartner, a proponent of the behavioral approach to studying entrepreneurship, prepared a comprehensive comparison of the major literature on the entrepreneur and entrepreneurship as he found it in 1988.[41] The comparison included attempts of various researchers to define an "entrepreneur" and/or "entrepreneurship," a description of the samples used by the researchers and a summary of the "characteristics" of entrepreneurs noted by the researchers. Gartner's list of the major shortcomings of work through that date included the following: a wide range of definitions of "the entrepreneur," many of which Gartner judged

---

[41] Gartner, W. Spring 1988. "'Who is an Entrepreneur?' Is the Wrong Question." *American Journal of Small Business* 12, no. 4, pp. 11–32, 13–20.

to be "vague," were used and it was not uncommon for researchers to neglect including any definition at all; few of the studies used the same definition of "the entrepreneur"; the samples of "entrepreneurs" were far from homogenous, a finding Gartner attributed to the inability to reach agreement on a definition of "the entrepreneur"; and the number of traits and characteristics attributed to entrepreneurs were full of contradictions and any "psychological profile" based on those traits and characteristics would portray a person that Gartner described as "larger than life" and "a sort of generic 'Everyman.'"[42]

---

[42] Id. at pp. 12 and 21.

CHAPTER 2

Role of Entrepreneurs in Launching New Businesses

Introduction

Gartner argued that the preferred path for studying entrepreneurship was to focus not on the person (the "entrepreneur") but on what he called "the primary phenomenon of entrepreneurship—the creation of organizations, the process by which new organizations come into existence."[1] Gartner referred to this as a "behavioral approach," which called for treating the organization as the primary level of analysis and concentrating on the complex process of creating a new organization, a process that was influenced by a number of factors including the activities undertaken by the entrepreneur to help the organization come into existence. Gartner explained: "The personality characteristics of the entrepreneur are ancillary to the entrepreneur's behaviors. Research on the entrepreneur should focus on what the entrepreneur does and not who the entrepreneur is."[2] Gartner noted that the behavioral approach was not new and that others, such as Cole, had argued that an entrepreneur should be seen as an "economic agent" who unites and reconstitutes all the necessary means of production (e.g., labor, capital, and property provided by others) to generate value that can be used to provide all of the stakeholders who have

---

[1] Gartner, W.B. Spring 1988. "'Who is an Entrepreneur?' Is the Wrong Question." *American Journal of Small Business* 21, no. 4, pp. 11–32 (citing Vesper, K. 1982. "Introduction and Summary of Entrepreneurship Research." In *Encyclopedia of Entrepreneurship*, eds. C. Kent, D. Sexton and K. Vesper, xxxi–xxxviii. Englewood Cliffs: Prentice-Hall).

[2] Id.

contributed inputs to the new venture with rewards such as wages, interest, and rent and also produce profits as the entrepreneur's own reward.[3]

Gartner was an outspoken critic of the "trait approach" to the study of entrepreneurship, and other advocates of the behavioral approach have been equally mindful of the shortcomings that have been identified with the trait approach. One commentator, Van de Ven, drew an interesting parallel between research on entrepreneurship and the evolution of research on leadership:

> Researchers wedded to the conception of entrepreneurship for studying the creation of organizations can learn much from the history of research on leadership. Like the studies of entrepreneurship, this research began by investigating the traits and personalities of leaders. However, no empirical evidence was found to support the expectation that there are a finite number of characteristics or traits of leaders and that these traits differentiate successful from unsuccessful leaders. Most recently, research into leadership has apparently made progress by focusing on the behavior of leaders (that is, one what they do instead of what they are) and by determining what situational factors or conditions moderate the effects of their behavior and performance.[4]

---

[3] Id. Gartner cited the following definition suggested by Cole, who himself relied on a quote from J.A. Say, that an entrepreneur is an economic agent who ". . . unites all means of production—the labor of the one, the capital or the land of the others—and who finds in the value of the products which result from their employment the reconstitution of the entire capital that he utilizes, and the value of the wages, the interest, and the rent which he pays, as well as the profits belonging to himself." Cole, A. 1946. "An Approach to the Study of Entrepreneurship: A Tribute to Edwin F. Gay." *The Tasks of Economic History Supplement VI of the Journal of Economic History* 3, pp. 1–15 (quoting Say, J. 1816. *A Treatise on Political Economy.* London: Sherwood, Neeley and Jones).

[4] Van de Ven, A.H. 1980. "Early Planning, Implementation and Performance of New Organizations." In *The Organization Life Cycle*, eds. J. Kimberly and R. Miles, 83–134, 86. San Francisco, CA: Jossey Bass (quoted in Gartner, W. Spring 1988. "'Who Is an Entrepreneur?' Is the Wrong Question." *American Journal of Small Business* 12, no. 4, pp. 11–32). For the further discussion of the study of

Role of the Entrepreneur in Creating New Organizations

In order to study the role of entrepreneurs in creating new organizations it is necessary to understand how organizations come into existence and then identify the roles that the entrepreneur plays in that process, the activities that the entrepreneur might be engaged in during the process, and the skills that the entrepreneur should acquire in order to be effective in that process. Gartner argued that a template for research was already available from the work carried out in the field of management studies with respect to identifying and understanding "what managers do" and suggested the following list of questions, many of which were adapted from the work of Mintzberg in his study of "managers,"[5] for researchers studying entrepreneurship[6]:

- What kinds of activities does the entrepreneur perform? What kinds of information does the entrepreneur process? Who does the entrepreneur work with and where and how frequently do these interactions occur?
- What are the distinguishing characteristics of the work performed by the entrepreneur? Specifically, what media does the entrepreneur use, what activities does the entrepreneur prefer to engage in, what is the flow of the entrepreneur's activities

---

the personal traits and characteristics of leaders, see "Leadership: A Library of Resources for Sustainable Entrepreneurs" prepared and distributed by the Sustainable Entrepreneurship Project (www.seproject.org).

[5] Mintzberg, H. 1973. *The Nature of Managerial Work*. New York, NY: Harper & Row. For a detailed discussion of Mintzberg's work on managerial roles, see "Management: A Library of Resources for Sustainable Entrepreneurs" prepared and distributed by the Sustainable Entrepreneurship Project (www.seproject.org).

[6] Gartner, W. Spring 1988. "'Who is an Entrepreneur?' Is the Wrong Question." *American Journal of Small Business* 12, no. 4, pp. 11–32, 27–28. Gartner noted that the answers to many of these questions were best pursued through field work that featured observations of entrepreneurs as they worked to create organizations and systematic description and classification of the observed activities of entrepreneurs. Id. at p. 27.

during the workday, how does the entrepreneur use his or
her time, and what are the pressures associated with the work
performed by the entrepreneur?

- What basic roles can be inferred from studying the activities
of entrepreneurs? What roles does the entrepreneur perform
with respect to collecting, analyzing, and distributing
information; decision making; and communicating and
dealing with people?

- What variations exist among the job activities of different
entrepreneurs and how can these variations be explained
(e.g., can they be attributed to the situation, the entrepreneur,
the job, the organization, and/or the environment)?

- To what extent is entrepreneurship a science? To what extent
is the work performed by an entrepreneur programmed
(i.e., the work is repetitive, systematic, and predictable)? To
what extent is the work of the entrepreneur programmable?

- What specific organizational creation skills does the entrepreneur need to have and how are those skills best acquired?[7]
Assuming that entrepreneurs are not born with these
skills, can they be learned through systematic training and
education? What role does prior experience as an entrepreneur play (i.e., is it possible to "learn as you go," as has been
suggested by some studies[8])? Are there any skills that are more

---

[7] With respect to this question see also Palmer, M. 1971. "The Application of
Psychological Testing to Entrepreneurial Potential." *California Management
Review* 13, no. 3, pp. 32–39.

[8] See, for example, Collins, O., and D. Moore. 1970. *The Organization Makers.*
New York, NY: Appleton-Century-Crofts; and Gartner, W. 1984. "Problems in
Business Startup: The Relationships Among Entrepreneurial Skills and Problem
Identification for Different Types of New Ventures." In *Frontiers of Entrepre-
neurship Research: The Proceedings of the Babson Conference on Entrepreneurship
Research*, eds. J. Hornaday, F. Tarpley, J. Timmons, and K. Vesper, 496–512.
Wellesley, MA: Babson College. See also Vesper, K. 1980. *New Venture Strategies.*
Englewood Cliffs, NJ: Prentice Hall (research suggests that entrepreneurs who
have already been involved in starting one organization tend to be more efficient
and successful in subsequent attempts to start new organizations).

important than others, such as identifying and evaluating problems?[9]

- Why do individuals decide to engage in the creation of a new organization? How do the founders of a new organization claim ownership rights and establish processes for communicating and working together as a team?[10]
- What skills and strategies do entrepreneurs use to identify and attract various types of support (e.g., financial, legal, marketing, and technological) needed for organizational creation to be successful? What role does business planning play and what are the features of successful business plans?[11]

Entrepreneurial Philosophies of Management

Gartner's list of questions provides a solid foundation for identifying and analyzing what entrepreneurs do in relation to the creation of new organizations. Another interesting alternative to the study of traits and characteristics examines entrepreneurship as an approach to managing an enterprise based on a fundamental strategy of identifying and pursuing opportunities in the firm's external environment without feeling limited by the actual resources that the firm currently has under its own control.[12]

---

[9] Researchers have suggested that a key to successful entrepreneurship is the ability to identify and prioritize problems. See, for example, Hoad, W., and P. Rosko. 1964. *Management Factors Contributing to the Success and Failure of New Small Manufacturers.* Ann Arbor: University of Michigan; and Lamont, L. 1972. "What Entrepreneurs Learn from Experience." *Journal of Small Business Management* 10, no. 3, pp. 36–41.

[10] With regard to team formation, see also Timmons, J. 1979. "Careful Analysis and Team Assessment can Aid Entrepreneurs." *Harvard Business Review* 57, no. 6, pp. 198–206.

[11] On this issue, see also Roberts, E. 1983. "Business Planning in the Startup High-Technology Enterprise." In *Frontiers of Entrepreneurship Research: The Proceedings of the 1983 Conference on Entrepreneurship Research,* eds. J. Hornaday, J. Timmons, and K. Vesper, 107–17. Wellesley, MA: Babson College.

[12] Stevenson, H. 1983. "A Perspective on Entrepreneurship." *Harvard Business School Note,* pp. 384-131. Sahlman and Stevenson took a similar approach in their definition of entrepreneurship as: ". . . a way of managing that involves

In order to understand how this "entrepreneurial behavior" works it is useful to compare the mindset and corresponding actions of "promoters" and "trustees" with respect to certain key dimensions of managerial activity. A promoter is someone who is comfortable assuming the risks and challenges of pursuing new business opportunities regardless of whether or not he or she currently controls the resources necessary for that pursuit to have a reasonable chance of success. On the other hand, the trustee falls at the opposite end of the spectrum and is continuously focused on efficient management and utilization of the firm's existing resources. Promoter-like behavior is typically associated with smaller firms while trustees and larger companies are similarly linked. The behavior within a single firm can, and usually does, evolves through time. As Cauthorn observed,

> [l]arge corporations [which] soon become risk-averting and cautious and are run, not by, innovating entrepreneurs, but by bureaucratic committees. These bureaucratized giants eliminate the entrepreneur and replace him or her with cautious and conservative managers who are, at best, maintainers.[13]

Contrasts between the behaviors of promoters and trustees can be seen along the following dimensions of managerial activity: strategic orientation, the strength and speed of commitment to the pursuit of opportunities, the resource commitment process, the attitude toward control over resources, management structure, and compensation and reward policies. We briefly examine each of these dimensions in the following paragraphs; however, at the outset it is useful to list the following

---

pursuing opportunity without regard to the resources currently controlled. Entrepreneurs identify opportunities, assemble required resources, implement a practical action plan, and harvest the reward in a timely, flexible way." Sahlman. W., and H. Stevenson. 1992. *Entrepreneurial Venture*. Boston, MA: Harvard Business School Publishing.

[13] Cauthorn, R.C. 1989. *Contributions to a Theory of Entrepreneurship*, 24. New York, NY: Garland Publishing, See also Burch, J.G. 1986. *Entrepreneurship*, 24. New York, NY: John Wiley & Sons (corporations tend to cease taking risks and are not run by entrepreneurs).

defining characteristics of the management philosophy of companies that can legitimately be classified as "entrepreneurial":

- Strategy is driven by the perception of opportunities available in the environment and is not constrained by concerns relating to a current lack of control over the resources necessary to pursue the identified opportunities.
- Once opportunities have been identified and the decision has been made to pursue them, actions will be taken quickly following consultation with a limited group of constituencies.
- Resources are committed to the pursuit of new opportunities in stages and each commitment is limited to the minimum amount of resources necessary at each stage or decision point in order to manage exposure and permit rapid withdrawal and redeployment of the resources.
- When resources are needed to pursue an opportunity it is sufficient to borrow, lease, or license those resources to complete the immediate action and defer acquisition of full control over such resources until the expense of the investment is justified.
- The optimal organizational structure is flat with minimal hierarchy and multiple direct information networks.
- The reward philosophy is value-driven, performance-based, and team-oriented.

As with many other aspects of the study of entrepreneurship there is no genuine agreement that entrepreneurs consistently apply some universal set of management principles to their pursuit of opportunities and innovation. In fact, it is difficult, if not impossible, to clearly and definitively analyze and explain the decision process of an entrepreneur who embarks on a path toward innovation. As one commentator put it, the "process is beyond systematic calculation."[14]

---

[14] Bull, I., and G.E. Willard. 1993. "Towards a Theory of Entrepreneurship." *Journal of Business Venturing* 8, no. 3, pp. 183–96, 188.

Strategic Orientation

The term "strategic orientation" can be thought of as the group of factors that are the primary drivers of the strategies adopted by a company. Firms led by founders and senior managers with a promoter-like mentality are most likely to design their strategies around opportunities that they identify in the relevant business environment with little or no concern for resource constraints. For example, promoters are likely to commit to developing a new product or technology that they believe will create a new market or transform an existing market even though they realize that they do not currently have the capital and other resources that are likely to be required in order to successfully complete the projected development effort. In contrast, the trustee-like mentality, often associated with larger firms, follows a resource-driven approach with respect to formulation of business strategy and focuses on how the resources that the firm currently controls can be efficiently managed and utilized. This type of approach shuns uncertainty and pushes managers to stick close to what is known and confine their strategic initiatives to incremental changes to, and realignment of, existing resources.

"Opportunistic" is a characteristic often incorporated into contemporary definitions of an entrepreneur and is usually accompanied by the terms "creative" and "innovative." It is important, however, to remember that opportunistic behavior may not involve striking out into new and relatively untested areas but could be a focus on finding new ways to combine existing ideas and/or apply existing ideas in a manner that is different from the status quo. While promoters may be oriented toward opportunistic behavior because of certain personality traits there are objective pressures in the environment of a firm that may push its strategic orientation in this direction. For example, conversion toward a promoter mentality may be dictated by the fact that trusteeship simply is no longer a viable strategy given that the opportunity streams that may have been available to the company in the past have dried up and there is no further value to be derived by tinkering with legacy products or technologies. A more entrepreneurial orientation may also be dictated by rapid and unexpected changes in technology, consumer requirements and spending habits, social values, and/or the regulatory environment. For example, technological breakthroughs inevitably create a degree of chaos in the marketplace as existing products suddenly become obsolete and new opportunities and expectations are created. Similarly, new regulatory requirements lead to revised product standards and often become a catalyst for developing new technologies and products.

It may be much easier for smaller, newly established firms to aggressively pursue opportunities without regard for resource constraints because they are not encumbered by some of the pressures that cause larger companies to become more administrative and conservative. For example, the managers of an established enterprise may feel an obligation to focus on deploying current resources as opposed to heading off into new directions that may require different and/or more people, new technologies, replacement of existing equipment, and aggressive capital-raising activities. Another issue that tends to reduce risk-taking behavior is that it is not encouraged by the firm's performance review and reward systems. At larger companies it is rare for managers to be punished for failing to pursue opportunities; however, their jobs are generally at risk if their efforts to take on an entrepreneurial project result in a downturn in traditional performance measures such as return on investment. Similarly, managers at big firms are usually selected and promoted for their ability to effectively utilize existing capacity and increase sales of current product lines.

Another interesting discussion that touches on differences in strategic orientation among traditional managers and entrepreneurs is the model created by Sarasvathy, which suggests that there are three forms of "thinking" or "reasoning" available to managers and that "entrepreneurial thinking" really is different from the others and can be taught.[15] Sarasvathy distinguished among the following forms:

- Managerial thinking, which is based on the causal reasoning normally taught to prospective entrepreneurs and managers and focuses on selecting between given means to achieve a predetermined goal.

---

[15] Sarasvathy, S. 2012. "What Makes Entrepreneurs Entrepreneurial?" http://entreprnr.net/assets/WhatMakesEntrepreneurs.pdf (accessed February 20, 2012).

- Strategic thinking, which is based on "creative" causal reasoning and focuses on generating new ways to achieve predetermined goals.
- Entrepreneurial thinking, which is based on effectual, not causal, reasoning and focusing on new ends using a given set of means.

Sarasvathy provided an interesting example of the contrast between causal and effectual reasoning taking an example of an entrepreneur who was a good Indian chef interested in starting a new business. An entrepreneur using causal reasoning would likely begin with the predetermined goal of starting an Indian restaurant and then go through the traditional steps of market definition and segmentation, targeting, and then positioning to reach customers who would enjoy and frequent the restaurant. In contrast, an entrepreneur using effectual reasoning would not start with the assumption that he or she would start an Indian restaurant but would instead gather up his or her means—who he or she is (i.e., traits, tastes, and abilities), what he or she knows (i.e., education, training, expertise, and experience), and whom he or she knows (i.e., social and professional networks)—and look for ways that those means can be employed in a profitable and enjoyable manner. This process begins with defining several possible markets, adding segments and/or strategic partners, defining the customer, and, finally, identifying how the needs of that customer can best be served by the means available to the entrepreneur. In the example provided by Sarasvathy, the entrepreneur may rent a location and start a restaurant but might also choose other paths such as partnering with an existing restaurant, participating in ethic food fairs, setting up a catering service, or cooking meals in his or her home and delivering them to office workers who have learned of the service through the entrepreneur's social and professional network.

A concept similar to strategic orientation is the proposed entrepreneurial characteristic of "innovativeness" suggested in the work of Mueller and Thomas. They noted that successful innovation requires more than just inventiveness but also demands commercialization of ideas, implementation, and the modification of existing products, systems, and resources. Success at "innovation" requires an entrepreneur who possesses the personal characteristics that reflect the necessary creativity and other skills to engage in "innovative behaviors," including the creation and implementation of competitive strategies to introduce new products and services and/or new methods of production, open new markets or sources of supply, or reorganize an entire industry.[16] Mueller and Thomas went on to cite the work of a number of researchers who provided empirical evidence for higher levels of "innovative preference" and "personal innovation" in entrepreneurs as opposed to managers and small business owners.[17]

Strength and Speed of Commitment to Pursuit of Opportunities

A strategic orientation toward new opportunities is one thing; however, the real test is the intensity with which the persons who see the opportunities press forward with the actual pursuit of the nascent business idea. A distinguishing characteristic of a promoter is his or her willingness to act quickly and assertively once a good opportunity is identified. In contrast, the trustee's thought and action process is one that is typically associated with large enterprises—very analytical with extensive internal discussion and negotiation within a relatively long decision-making process. The apparent tendency of the promoter to "jump right in" is sometimes seen as overly risky and impetuous; however, this perspective is simplistic and

---

[16] Mueller, S., and A. Thomas. 2000. "Culture and Entrepreneurial Potential: A Nine Country Study of Locus of Control and Innovativeness." *Journal of Business Venturing* 16, no. 1, pp. 51–75, 57 (citing Bird, B. 1989. *Entrepreneurial Behavior*. Glenview, IL: Scott Foresman; Carland, J., F. Hoy, W. Boulton, and J. Carland. 1984. "Differentiating Entrepreneurs from Small Business Owners: A Conceptualization." *Academy of Management Review* 9, no. 2, pp. 354–59).

[17] Id. (citing, for example, Carland, J.W., J.C. Carland, F. Hoy, and W. Boulton. 1998. "Distinctions Between Entrepreneurial and Small Business Ventures." *International Journal of Management* 5, no. 1 , pp. 98–103; Smith, N., and J. Miner. 1985. "Motivational Considerations in the Success of Technologically Innovative Entrepreneurs: Extended Sample Findings." In *Frontiers of Entrepreneurship Research*, eds. J. Hornaday, E. Shile, J. Timmons, and K. Vesper. Wellesley, MA: Babson College).

misleading in many cases because successful promoters are acting on the basis of their experience in the particular area in which the opportunity arises and their instinctive sense of the steps that will need to be taken in order to build a path where none seems to exist at the beginning.

Firms that demonstrate a more entrepreneurial approach to committing to the pursuit of new opportunities tend to display one or more specific characteristics. First, the promoter and other managers are action-oriented and this pushes the company to commit quickly to contacting and claiming the customers, employees, capital, and other resources that are necessary to take advantage of the opportunity. Second, these firms understand that many opportunities come with very short windows for making the market entry decision and that delay in acting will expose them to prohibitively high late entry costs, including the need to make significant investment to overcome the competitive and technological advantages of "first movers." Third, these companies are adroit at managing their limited resources in a way that allows them to both rapidly respond to new opportunities and withdraw quickly from projects that are not working out. Finally, the ability to quickly commit resources follows from the fact that entrepreneurial ventures have a limited number of constituencies that must be consulted before a decision is made. This allows those firms to be more flexible than larger and more hierarchical organizations that must go through extended deliberations and internal negotiations before they can move forward with a significant change in strategic direction.

In contrast, companies that are following the trustee model are slow to commit resources to new opportunities for several reasons. First, these firms, generally larger, have a number of internal and external constituencies that believe they should have a voice in strategic decisions. As a result no choices, much less a move into a new direction, can be made with complete a long and complicated process of consultation and negotiation, which inevitably leads to delays. In addition, the negotiation process typically requires a large number of concessions in order to garner the necessary support and the result is generally a much less aggressive approach to a specific opportunity. In fact, this is one of the main reasons that most of the new strategic initiatives of larger firms tend to focus on incremental or evolutionary changes in existing products and technologies rather than on projects designed to effect revolutionary change. The decision-making process at large firms with a trustee mentality will also slowed by the strong emphasis on risk analysis that accompanies the determination of strategy. Finally, any decision made by the trustee will need to take into account the current resources of the firm and the resulting strategy will often be skewed toward assuring that existing personnel and related assets will remain deployed. While this is a noble objective, particularly when the goal is to continue offering jobs to loyal employees, it can significantly impair the flexibility of the firm and its ability to respond to new opportunities that will ultimately require resources that are not currently controlled.

Process of Committing Resources

Another distinguishing factor between promoters and trustees is the approach that they follow with respect to commitment of resources to the pursuit of a new opportunity. As noted above, the strategic orientation of a promoter is driven by a willingness to commit to an opportunity with accepting as a constraint the lack of current control over resources that may be needed in the future. This mindset drives the promoter to view commitment of resources to a new project as a multistep process in which additional resources will only be committed at key decision points along the way and the amount of each additional commitment will be limited to what is necessary in order to progress to the next milestone. In contrast, trustees are generally unwilling to take on a new project unless and until an extensive analysis of the required resources has been completed and all of the resources thought to be necessary for the success of the project have been identified and formally allocated to the project. Promoters are more willing to minimize the resources committed to a particular project and focus on maximizing the value that the firm is able to create using those resources; however, there is necessarily a higher level of risk associated with this approach since unforeseen problems may arise at a future decision point in gathering the additional resources necessary to continue. The size and stage of development of the promoter firm often has a lot to do with this approach. A small company at the startup stage generally has few resources available for any project and its ability to obtain additional resources, particularly capital, will depend on the success of its efforts in the early phases of a new project. In addition, the best opportunities generally appear in dynamic environments where technologies and standards have yet to fully emerge and staged commitment of resources provides promoters with the flexibility to choose from the best available resources at each point in the decision process rather than being locked into a commitment to use a manufacturing process that is no longer cost-effective or a technology that has become obsolete because of advances in other areas of the environment while the promoter firm has been working through its own development process.

Trustees are more comfortable with a one-time commitment of all of the resources required for a particular project for several reasons. First, managers in a trustee-oriented organization tend to have a much higher level of personal risk avoidance and are typically reluctant to commit to a long-term project without comfort that sufficient resources have already been set aside to satisfy the requirements that have been identified at the beginning of the project. Second, when excess resources are available for use it is easier for managers to obtain the short-term return on investment that is valued within the performance and compensation structures of larger companies. Third, the planning and budgeting systems used by trustee-type organizations are usually set up for single decisions after an extended period of internal analysis, discussion, and negotiation as discussed before. As a result, proponents of a new project are pushed toward seeking approval for the largest amount of resources possible before the project begins. If they attempt to spread the commitment of new resources over multiple stages the project will likely bog down at each decision point with a resultant loss of momentum and advantage in relation to competitors.

Control of Resources

Resources are necessary for the pursuit of any new opportunity; however, promoters and trustees diverge significantly with respect to their attitudes regarding the manner and degree of control over the resources—capital, personnel, technology, and equipment—necessary in order to execute the appropriate strategy for a given opportunity. Promoters focus primarily on the ability to use a given resource only to the extent necessary in order to achieve specifically identified immediate goals and objectives. Promoters are not interested in taking on the additional costs and risks of excess capacity, which is often the case when a resource is bought rather than simply borrowed or leased, and thus are slow to commit to building in-house resources that may be more difficult to jettison or redirect as new the environment changes and opportunities come and go. On the other hand, trustees, consistent with the reluctance explained above to commit to a new project unless all the resources have been identified in advance, have a strong preference for own or actually employing all of the tangible, intangible, and human resources necessary for new projects and day-to-day business activities.

The promoter's approach to resource control is based on several supporting beliefs and strategic operating principles. First, promoters recognize the movement toward increased resource specialization, particularly when pursuing opportunities in dynamic market, and this means that the most prudent way to reduce risks and control the level of fixed costs is to bring in the required specialist personnel and assets—design engineers or customized testing equipment—for a limited period of time and tightly constrained assignments. Second, leasing rather than buying provides a hedge against unexpected obsolescence, which as explained above can occur quickly when technologies and standards are in a state of flux. Third, the ability to eliminate unnecessary resources quickly, by exercising built-in options to terminate leases or licenses, creates flexibility and allows the promoter to free up capital easily and redirect it quickly as needed. In contrast, established companies generally apply a trustee mentality to resource control for various reasons. For example, resource control is an important indicator of status, authority, and compensation for larger firms and managers have business, political, and psychological incentives to "purchase" and maintain control over resources. In addition, it is easier to coordinate the execution of projects if all the resources have already been identified and appropriated and ready for deployment; however, these advantages should be weighed against the risk that some resources may not be fully utilized prior to the time that they are actually needed for a particular project. Finally, larger firms are more likely to adopt stockpiling strategies for core resources as a hedge against sudden shortages in the marketplace. As such, it is common practice for managers to accumulate buffer inventories and proactively seek control over key business relationships with suppliers and distributors. Control of resources through ownership is also seen as important mode of defense against preemption by competitors.

Management Structure

In order for the promoter to be able to make the various decisions regarding pursuit of opportunities and control of resources he or she must have immediate and direct access to all relevant information from within the organizational structure of the company. Accordingly, it is not surprising that the preferred management structure for the promoter is flat with multiple information networks and direct connections between the promoter and each of the key internal stakeholders involved in developing and implementing the strategy relating to specific opportunities. While entrepreneurs are often stereotyped as being eccentric inventors interested more in ideas than in execution the reality is that the most successful entrepreneurs are those who have the management skills to coordinate the use of key resources that are not under the direct control of their companies, which means constantly communicating and negotiating with external resource controllers.[18] A flat organization also maximizes flexibility, which is important in the dynamic environments in which the development of new opportunities occurs. In addition, a nonhierarchical organizational structure is consistent with the need of creative and innovative employees to have some level of independence to freely pursue their ideas without having to overcome the problems that often delay activities in companies that have become too bureaucratic.[19]

---

[18] It is widely believed that entrepreneurs lack critical management skills. See, for example, Burch, J.G. 1986. *Entrepreneurship*, 24. New York, NY: John Wiley & Sons (entrepreneurs are good at starting companies and making them successful, but not at managing them).

[19] For further discussion, see "Organizational Design: A Library of Resources for Sustainable Entrepreneurs" prepared and distributed by the Sustainable Entrepreneurship Project (www.seproject.org).

A larger firm often has difficulty shifting toward an entrepreneurial orientation because of the management structure that has evolved as the company has grown and matured. The normal pressure on the growing business is toward a formalized hierarchy with a gradually increasing number of managerial levels that tend to increase the distance between the leaders of the company—the members of the senior management group—and the employees who are closest to the potential sources of new opportunities (e.g., customers or suppliers). As a result, the information systems for a trustee-type organization are different than those in a promoter-type firm. Larger companies are more interested in reports that allow senior managers to fulfill the challenges of monitoring and coordinating a diverse range of resources—in other words, controlling the actions of employees at all levels of the hierarchy. The need for control also underlies efforts to clearly define authority and responsibility within the organizational structure and develop and enforce policies and procedures to standardize the response of managers and employees to frequently occurring events. Finally, reward systems in larger firms typically create incentives for managers to broaden their span of control over resources.

Compensation and Reward Policies

There are sharp distinctions between promoter- and trustee-oriented firms with respect to their philosophies regarding rewards and compensation. Promoter-type companies focus heavily on "value creation" and tie compensation to performance on activities that are closely related to the creation of value for the firm's stakeholders. This approach is consistent with the expectations of individuals who tend to be drawn to entrepreneurial ventures—they are more independent and believe strongly that they should be rewarded based on their individual contributions as opposed to how long they have been with the company or where there specific position sits within a formal organizational chart. In fact, companies seeking to recruit the human resources necessary to successfully tackle truly innovative opportunities must be prepared to offer performance-based rewards packages. The type of external financial support sought and obtained by promoters—venture capital—also pushes their companies toward creation and distribution of value since these investors expect and demand high and quick return on their investments.

Larger companies with a trustee-type orientation have come under increasing criticism regarding their seeming inability to maximize value from their operations and distribute that value to their shareholders in the form of dividends and stronger performance in the stock markets. In fact, shareholder dissatisfaction has become so strong that perceived failures with respect to value creation have led to "forced" acquisitions of poorly performing firms and accelerated turnover among chief executive officers. There are several reasons that make it difficult for a large company to move toward a performance-based compensation system. First of all, as firms grow loyalty and tenure inevitably creep in as factors in compensation and promotion decisions and this creates difficulties in adopting alternatives that might reward high-performing newcomers while penalizing others who have stuck with the company for years and been "loyal soldiers." Second, since there are so many people involved in specific activities within larger companies it can be extremely difficult to isolate, measure, and reward individual performance. Finally, managers seeking long-term tenure at larger firms tend to err on the side of conservatism and make decisions with a strong eye on protecting their positions and scope of authority and avoiding actions that might be "career ending" within the context of the particular firm.

CHAPTER 3

Founder's Traits and Skills

Founder's Personality Traits

Founders start businesses for a number of reasons, as discussed below, and it is difficult to identify a set of personality traits that can associated with everyone who starts a new business. In fact, a fair number of businesses are started for reasons not chosen by the founder, such as when the founder loses his or her job with an employer. Putting aside these "accidental" or "reluctant" founders, however, it is useful to explore some of the research that has been done on the personality traits of founders and most of the work in this area has been done by researchers interested in the overall phenomenon of "entrepreneurship."[1] This is not surprising given that in recent years entrepreneurs, such as Bill Gates and the late Steve Jobs, have assumed almost mythical positions in the eyes of the public and entrepreneurs in general have come to be referred to as "the hero[s] of capitalism and the free enterprise system."[2]

In his 1911 classic work titled *The Theory of Economic Development*, legendary economist Joseph A. Schumpeter provided the following description of his views regarding the psychology of the entrepreneur:

> Entrepreneurs . . . are not propelled solely by a wish to grow rich or by any "motivation of the hedonist kind." Instead, they feel "the will to conquer: the impulse to fight, to prove oneself superior to others, to succeed for the sake, not of the fruits of success,

---

[1] For further discussion of research on the personality traits of entrepreneurs, see "Entrepreneurship: A Library of Resources for Sustainable Entrepreneurs" prepared and distributed by the Sustainable Entrepreneurship Project (www.seproject.org).

[2] Burch, J.G. 1986. *Entrepreneurship*, 24. New York, NY: John Wiley & Sons.

but of success itself . . . There is the joy of creating, of getting
things done, or simply of exercising one's energy and ingenuity."[3]

It is important to realize that entrepreneurship was a novel, and relatively ignored, concept during Schumpeter's lifetime and he lacked a body of
empirical data that he could use to prove and support his ideas. As time has
passed, however, Schumpeter's views about economic progress and the role
of the entrepreneur have been widely praised and embraced as prophetic.

Attempting to identify the personality traits most commonly found
among entrepreneurs has become one of the most popular areas of
academic research.[4] A basic survey of the literature uncovers the following
as the most commonly mentioned traits:

- A need for achievement, which goes beyond mere monetary
  awards to include a drive to establish and build a growing
  business;
- A high internal locus of control or a need among
  entrepreneurs to be their own bosses;
- A high propensity for risk-taking and ability to absorb and
  learn from failure[5];
- A need for independence, which sometimes is evidenced
  by an inability to fit into a more traditional, or large, firm
  situation[6]; and

---

[3] See Schumpeter, J.A. 1934. *The Theory of Economic Development: An Inquiry
into Profits, Capital, Credit, Interest, and the Business Cycle (translated by Redvers
Opie)*. Cambridge, MA: Harvard University Press.

[4] For a more detailed discussion of the personal motivational traits of entrepreneurs, see "Entrepreneurship: A Library of Resources for Sustainable Entrepreneurs" prepared and distributed by the Sustainable Entrepreneurship Project
(www.seproject.org).

[5] See, for example, Burch, J.G. 1986. *Entrepreneurship*, 33. New York, NY: John
Wiley & Sons ("[f]ew, if any entrepreneurs have escaped failure").

[6] See, for example, Gilder, G. 1984. *The Spirit of Enterprise*, 132. New York,
NY: Simon and Schuster ("[t]he fastest-growing new firms often arise through
defections of restive managers and engineers from large corporations or through
the initiatives of immigrants and outcasts beyond the established circles of commerce"), 247 (entrepreneurship arises in "rebellion against established firms"),

- A predisposition toward innovative behavior, including creativity, vision, and capacity to inspire.

Cauthorn has written that "[f]or thinking innovatively, imagination is more important than knowledge" and has noted that "[l]ogic alone points away from entrepreneurial activity."[7] Kirzner noted that while successful entrepreneurship is, to a degree, a function of "luck," entrepreneurs make what appear to be unforeseen discoveries because they are alert to new opportunities and act in systematic ways based on their hunches or vision.[8] In addition, while many of the traits listed above describe some sort of displacement as the catalyst for a person's pursuit of entrepreneurship, Shapero and Sokol rightly point out that only some people can turn a displacement into an opportunity.[9] Shapero and Sokol have also mentioned that entrepreneurs are often influenced and inspired by mentors.[10]

Clearly the words that Schumpeter wrote almost 100 years ago were prophetic and anticipated much of what psychologists, anthropologists, and sociologists are finding today. However, while all this is quite interesting, it has created a good deal of controversy since it suggests that entrepreneurs are most likely to be born and not made. If that is the case, universities should stop offering classes and degrees in entrepreneurship and governments should shift their funding activities from training to investments in improving the environment within which these "special personalities" can perform. A more reasonable interpretation of the data is that the presence of these traits in a particular person can be used as measure of the likelihood that he or she will *voluntarily* choose an entrepreneurial path. This leaves open the possibility that entrepreneurship can be an acquired talent and recognizes that, as mentioned above, unforeseen

---

and 257 (entrepreneurship is an "irrational process" carried on by "orphans and outcasts").

[7] Cauthorn, R.C. 1989. *Contributions to a Theory of Entrepreneurship*, 28 and 32. New York, NY: Garland Publishing.

[8] Kirzner, I.M. 1979. *Perception, Opportunity, and Profit*, 180–81. Chicago: The University of Chicago Press.

[9] See, for example, Shapero, A., and L. Sokol. 1982. "The Social Dimensions of Entrepreneurship." In *Encyclopedia of Entrepreneurship*, eds. C.A. Kent, D.L. Sexton and K.H. Vesper, 74. Englewood Cliffs, NJ: Prentice Hall.

[10] Id.

circumstances, such as sudden job loss due to downsizing and offshoring, often turn loyal, long-term employees of large firms into unexpected entrepreneurs. Even more important to remember is that even if someone possesses the energy, creativity, and ability to persevere linked to the entrepreneurial ideal it does not mean that he or she will be successful in launching and managing a business and this brings us to the topic in the next section: the founder's skills inventory.

Founder's Skills Inventory

While starting and operating a business, particularly a business that is expected to grow rapidly, is a team effort, members of the founding team should not move forward too quickly without closely and carefully analyzing and evaluating their own personal skills, strengths, and weaknesses and then comparing them to the skills and other attributes that are expected to be necessary in order to successfully operate the chosen business (see Table 3.1). If a founder is not strong in a particular area, he or she must be mindful of the fact that the weakness needs to be

Table 3.1 Assessment of personal characteristics of prospective founders

- Are you self-motivated (i.e., a "self-starter") and able to persevere and keep yourself moving forward and try new solutions?
- Do you believe in yourself and feel confident about your professional and personal skills and your ability to leverage them successfully in your new business?
- Are you willing to work harder than you've ever worked before and for long hours without the security of a steady paycheck and no promise of ultimate success?
- Are you healthy and do you have a regular program of exercise and diet in place that will sustain your energy level?
- Are you willing to take responsibility for situations, make tough decisions on your own, and accept the risks of failure with respect to such decisions?
- Are you creative and innovative and consistently able to find new ways of doing things?
- Do you know your strengths and weaknesses?
- Have you identified the values—honesty, service, quality, innovation, teamwork—that you believe will be most important for the operation and success of your business and have you prepared a brief description of how each of the chosen values will be used in the business?
- Do you know what is really important to you and are you clear about the ethical values you will refer to when making decisions about your business and your actions?

addressed by recruiting qualified individuals to work with the business, either as an additional member of founding team or as an employee or key outside consultant. While introspection necessarily takes time away from the work necessary to launch a new venture, entrepreneurs should be encouraged to undertake some type of formal assessment of their personal characteristics and organizational and managerial skills that includes hard and pointed questions about their motives for embarking on an entrepreneurial path. In addition to the questions included in this chapter, a wide range of resources are available for assessment. For example, a *Wall Street Journal* article on entrepreneurship suggested that persons considering self-employment and launching a new business ask themselves the following questions and ask their associates to critically evaluate their answers[11]:

- Are you willing and able to bear great financial risk?
- Are you willing to sacrifice your lifestyle for potentially many years?
- Is your "significant other" on board?
- Do you like all aspects of running a business?
- Are you comfortable making decisions on the fly with no playbook?
- What's your track record of executing your ideas?
- How persuasive and "well spoken" are you?
- Do you have a concept that you are passionate about?
- Are you a self-starter?
- Do you have a business partner?

A wide variety of necessary professional skills for launching a new business have been identified (see Table 3.2); however, it is fair to say that most of them can probably be fit into the following categories.

Sales and Marketing Skills

The goal for any new business is to flourish through the sale of products and services and thus it is not surprising that one of the most important

---

[11] Spors, K. February 23, 2009. "So You Want to Be an Entrepreneur." *The Wall Street Journal.*

Table 3.2 Assessment of organizational and managerial skills of prospective founders

- Do you have the business skills you need to run a business?
- Do you have managerial experience?
- Have you worked in a business like the one you want to start?
- Have you thoroughly researched your business and its industry?
- Do you have the technical skills you will need to operate your particular business?
- Have you evaluated your experience and talents with respect to the key skills and knowledge necessary for operating a business—planning, product or service knowledge, financial management and budgeting, marketing, sales, and recruitment and management of human resources?
- Have you created a plan for obtaining information or assistance with respect to those skills and knowledge as to which you lack experience and/or talent?
- Do you have business partners or advisors who can compensate for your weaknesses?
- Are you a good planner and do you have the vision to see in advance the steps and tasks that it takes to get something done?
- Are you a good listener and do you take the time to listen to and really understand what others may be thinking or feeling?
- Can you deal effectively with other people and do you enjoy maintaining relations with others?
- Are you an effective leader, motivator, and communicator?
- Are you willing to delegate authority and responsibility to others?
- Do you project a professional image to your customers and other business partners?
- Can people trust what you say and that you will do what you say you will do?
- Do you have the skills and other resources necessary to perform an adequate feasibility study of the key concepts underlying your idea for a new business?
- Have you established and follow a plan for continuously monitoring events and changes in your target market?
- Do you belong to a trade association or other business organization that provides you with opportunities to meet with other entrepreneurs and executives in your industry?
- Do you belong to local clubs and organizations that provide opportunities to meet prospective business partners and create a positive image in your community?

areas for a prospective business owner to consider is his or her skills with respect to sales and marketing. In addition to the ability to set and execute sales and marketing strategies, the founder will need to be able to manage a group of sales representatives and communicate with customers to handle complaints and solicit feedback on the company's products and services. The founder will also be involved in launching and managing advertising campaigns and negotiations with prospective distributors. Other sales and marketing activities that will typically occupy a good deal of a founder's time include competitive analysis, developing marketing plans, and pricing and packaging.

Financial Management Skills

Many prospective business owners find themselves unequipped to deal with preparation of budgets and financial statements. This is one of the main reasons that a controller or chief financial officer is one of the first positions to be filled on the management team as the business grows. Beyond that, the founder should be prepared to understand and handle billing procedures, negotiations with vendors and customers regarding payments and credit terms, and tax payment and reporting requirements.

Human Resource Skills

While most persons who voluntarily launch a new business have a high degree of self-motivation and are often seen to be "loners," they need to understand that they cannot succeed without the help of others and that they will need to assume the role of an employer and provide leadership and motivation to the company's human resources. While the founder may have exceptional vision regarding the creation and implementation of new products and technologies, he or she often has little or no background in managing other people. Prospective business owners need to think about whether they are a good judge of people. The founder also needs to consider whether he or she is able and willing to train employees and communicate his or her vision for the business. Finally, the founder must be prepared for the unpleasant task of disciplining and firing employees.

Organizational and Management Skills

The founder's organizational and management skills should also be evaluated. It is one thing to develop an innovative technology, product, or service; however, the work will generally be of little importance unless the founder has the discipline to develop a long-term strategic plan for the business and establish realistic goals and milestones. New business owners often run into trouble in delegating specific tasks to others in the organization. However, it is essential that they strike the proper balance between directing employees and leaving them free to pursue the best method for achieving a particular objective. In many cases, none of the founders have the management skills necessary to grow the business beyond a certain point and outside investors will require that the company hire an experienced chief executive officer to run the company. If this is anticipated, how does the founder expect that he or she will react to an "outsider" joining the business at such a senior level?

Stress Management Skills

Starting a new business can be a stressful experience and the prospective business owner needs to carefully and candidly assess his or her ability to manage risk and, possibly, failure. He or she needs to be prepared for long hours and hopefully will have the capacity to both work alone and interact well with other founders and the key initial employees of the new venture. It is also important for founders to have the support of their families in the effort.

Nassif et al. studied entrepreneurship from a dynamic perspective in order to gain a better understanding of the values, characteristics, and actions over time as they launch and develop their businesses.[12] They referred to various statistics regarding the importance of small- and medium-sized businesses to the Brazilian economy in terms of revenues and jobs; however, they also reported on the high mortality rate among those businesses and observed that one of the main reasons for failure was the inability of Brazilian entrepreneurs to effectively develop and manage their businesses. Based on their analysis of work by various researchers on the types and characteristics of Brazilian small business entrepreneurs, Nassif et al. developed an entrepreneurial process dynamics framework that included and distinguished "affective aspects," which were most important during the earliest stages of the entrepreneurial process, and "cognitive aspects," which became more important relative to the affective aspects as time went on and the business matured. Affective aspects included perseverance, courage, will power, initiative, willingness to take risks, personal motivation,

---

[12] Nassif, V., A. Ghobril, and N. Siqueira da Silva. April/June 2010. "Understanding The Entrepreneurial Process: A Dynamic Approach." *Brazilian Administrative Review* 7, no. 2.

facing challenges, passion for the business, autonomy, self-confidence, and independence. Cognitive aspects included assumption of calculated risks, ability to establish partnerships, defining goals and planning skills, knowing one's limits, and eloquent communication skills.

Are You a Scale-Up Entrepreneur?

One of the fundamental conditions for growth-oriented entrepreneurship is the desire of the entrepreneurs who are the members of the founding team to not only launch and navigate their businesses to the point of survival but to go beyond that to enjoy significant growth in revenues, employment, and market impact. Isenberg and others have argued that the skills necessary to get through the startup phase, while being obviously crucial, are not the same as those that entrepreneurs need to "scale up" the business to the point where growth engines are mobilized. Isenberg developed a simple set of assessment questions that entrepreneurs could peruse to determine whether they were "cut out to be a scale-up entrepreneur." These questions were based on interviews that Isenberg conducted with scale-up entrepreneurs from around the world and suggest that backgrounds and actions associated with success in moving through the risky launch stage of a new business to the point where scaling is feasible. Specifically, entrepreneurs should make a note of whether they "agree" or "disagree" with the following statements:

- Something inside compels me to make something that will impact the marketplace.
- I am great at selling things to people that they may not know they want, nor think they have the money to buy.
- I have people on my team who are better than me in several areas of knowledge or practice.
- My venture already has the procedures, policies, and processes in place to be ten times the size we are today.
- When I don't know what my next step is, I have experienced people I can turn to for ideas.
- There is money out there to fuel a venture that is growing fast; I just have to find it when I am ready.
- When I achieve my objectives I keep raising the bar higher and higher.
- I am one of the best sales people I know.
- Think big; thinking small is a crime.
- I know entrepreneurs just like me who have grown big, fast.
- The sales process is just starting when the customer first says no.
- If my venture stands in one place too long, it runs the risk of perishing. We have to keep moving forward.
- I know how to find great people to hire.
- Nothing gives me a bigger rush than closing a big sale.
- It is more important to know of a big problem that customers have and then look for a solution, than it is to have a solution that is looking for important problems to solve.
- I used to think our great technology would take us to leadership in our market—now I realize it is our team, our organization, our marketing and our ambition to sell.
- Even though I am a startup, I think more like a market leader than a small business.

The greater the number of times that one "agreed" with a statement, the more likely that he or she had the motivation to scale up their new venture. Two important themes were emphasized when compiling the questions: persistence and experience in all aspects of selling (e.g., sales organization, compensation, pipeline management, and selling skills) and attitude, particularly the ambition to grow the business and a vision for the business that is grand and large.

While sales is one of the most important skills for a scale up entrepreneurs, others areas for which founding teams might seek out training including personal leadership, effective communication, project management, managing performance, selecting a winning team, negotiation and managing change.

Sources: Isenberg, D. March 24, 2013. "Find Out if You're a Scale-Up Entrepreneur with this Two-Minute Test." *Harvard Business Review.* See also Isenberg, D. July 2013. *Worthless, Impossible, and Stupid: How Contrarian Entrepreneurs Create and Capture Extraordinary Value.* Cambridge MA: Harvard Business Press. Suggestions for training program for scale up entrepreneurs are available from the "School for Scale-Up" offered through the Cambridge Network.

Reasons for Starting the New Business

Men and women who think of themselves as entrepreneurs sometimes don't take the time to understand how or why they ended up doing what they are trying to do. In fact, taking a moment to step back and contemplate is sometimes seen as antientrepreneurial since it isn't spontaneous, proactive, or creative. Nonetheless, the founders of a startup venture that seems to be continuously challenged by various issues and hurdles should perhaps stop for a moment to consider what is driving their foray into entrepreneurship. For example, they should ask whether their interest lies in creating a new process or method, discovering and penetrating a new market, leveraging economies of scale and flexibility, or simply escaping the drudgery of working at a large firm. The answer to this question can have a significant impact on the decisions that are made regarding the strategies and values of the firm and the priorities established by attracting resources to the venture.

People start new businesses for a number of different reasons including a simple passion for entrepreneurship, dissatisfaction with the decision of a current employer not to invest in a particular product or service, or economic necessity due to the need to generate income following loss of a job with another firm. The selection of the type of business also varies depending on various factors including the background and skills of the founders, suggestions from prospective business partners, and trends that appear to be popular based on media reports. In order for business planning to be useful and successful it is important for the founders to take a little time to explore the process that each of them followed in selecting the particular business. Each founder should ponder his or her motivations and goals individually and then the entire group of founders should meet to discuss the reasons for launching the new venture and what each of them hopes to see accomplished from the effort. Outside advisors should be brought into the discussion since they are often better positioned to provide objective input and identify potential flaws in the logic or conflicts among the founders. Among the questions that should be posed and discussed are the following:

- What was the driving force behind the selection of the type of business? It is all well and good to want to convert a preexisting hobby or interest into a commercial venture; however, the venture is likely to fail if there is not sufficient demand for the product or service.
- Have the founders devoted sufficient time to planning the new venture? It is not enough to have a good idea or identify a new market opportunity. The founders must be able to carefully consider competitive factors and their ability to gather the resources that will be required to enter and exploit the market.
- Have the founders sought advice from others who operate the same or similar businesses? Many businesses fail because the founders were unwilling to ask for help in getting things up and running or were unable to find the information on the tasks that need to be mastered to make the business a success. If the founders do not know how to get this information, they should consider contacting the local chamber of commerce or trade associations that include managers and professionals involved in the target business area.
- Do the founders have the requisite experience to conduct the particular business? In many cases, a founder will have had an extensive career working with companies involved in

the development and promotion of the specific product or service. But, if that is not the case, he or she should consider the effects of inexperience on the venture. The founders may be planning on recruiting managers and other employees who can provide the appropriate skills and contacts. Another possibility to consider is working for someone else for a limited period of time in order to gain the necessary experience and training.

Advantages and Disadvantages of Business Ownership

Before a person decides to launch his or her own business, careful consideration should be given to some of the important pros and cons of starting and building a new venture. Commitment is a key factor and the founder (and members of his or her family) needs to be prepared to sacrifice a good deal of personal time and, in many cases, place his or her financial security at risk. While founders may enjoy having the chance to operate their own business, they should not forget the possibility that they will have to perform a few unpleasant tasks, such as terminating employees.

Earnings Potential

If things go well, the new business owner will likely have the opportunity to earn more money that he or she could make when working for someone else. But, this is not universally true and some of the nonfinancial factors described below may be more important in a particular situation.

Autonomy and Responsibility

Autonomy and responsibility are often driving factors for someone wanting to start his or her own business. He or she will have a chance to be their own boss and make all the crucial decisions that might determine the success or failure of the business. In turn, these responsibilities, if well executed, can provide the founder with a great sense of personal satisfaction and fulfillment.

Supervisory and Mentoring Opportunities

The founder will have a chance to supervise and educate others about his or her vision for the particular product or service that the company is offering. Many founders find this aspect of the business to be quite satisfying; however, others have little patience for dealing with employees.

Job Security

Many people feel that by launching their own business, they would not have to worry about being fired. Well, that may be true in the early stages; however, if the business requires outside capital it is certain that the founders will need to learn to be accountable to their investors.

Skill Development

As the boss, he or she will be able to get involved in every aspect of the business and gain experience in a variety of functional disciplines. Many would-be entrepreneurs may be frustrated at larger companies if they are not allowed to be active outside of their particular department or group. While many people are interested in founding a new business in order to get involved in new disciplines, they should not underestimate the demands of the need to develop knowledge in so many different areas at once. It is not uncommon for a new business owner to be called on to make decisions in such diverse areas as accounting and bookkeeping, inventory control, production planning, advertising and promotion, and market research. It is the rare person that can pull that off successfully over an extended period of time.

Community Involvement

Many founders view starting their own business as an opportunity to get involved with their community and contribute directly to the well-being of the local economy and the employees and customers that reside in the neighborhood. This is obviously a fine and noble objective; however, the founder must also develop a strategy for generating sufficient return on his or her investment to maintain the viability of the venture.

Financial Risk

It is the rare case where starting a new business does not entail substantial financial risk to the founder (and his or her family). Of course, the risk may be warranted in light of the expected return; however, it is important to make sure that enough financial resources are available to meet the personal needs of the founder and get the business up and running.

Time Commitment

A new venture is hard work and founders should expect to work long hours and forgo opportunities for vacations and recreational activities during the early months and years of the new venture.

Resources

Persons eager to start their own business sometimes forget the value of the resources and assistance that may be available in a larger enterprise. The new venture generally cannot afford the support staff who can free the founder from the time involved in tending to administrative details of the business. Initially, income from the business may not be as steady as the founder hoped for and in some cases he or she may have little or no income at all. The founder needs to be sure that he or she has enough savings and/or other sources of income to get through the rough periods.

Advantages and Disadvantages of Acquiring an Existing Business

Starting a business from scratch can be a daunting undertaking, and some fledgling entrepreneurs prefer to purchase an existing business instead. As with any business decision, there are pros and cons that should be considered when looking at a possible acquisition of a business that has been up and running and the entrepreneurs should carefully consider both the positive aspects and the problems that may crop up after the deal is done and the seller has moved on.

One obvious advantage of acquiring an existing business is the ability that the new owners can get operations up and running immediately. However, purchasing an existing business may require more startup capital than might be the case if the buyer had simply started a new business from scratch. The buyer may be forced to pay for assets that were not wanted or that were not expected to be needed until much later in the development of the business. The new owner may also find that the company's fixed assets and equipment must be replaced in order to effectively pursue any new business goals.

The buyer will obviously hope that existing inventory and receivables will result in a steady short-term stream of cash that can be used to expand the business. However, while existing inventory will, hopefully, be a source of revenue for the new owner, it is sometimes the case that inventory items are obsolete and must be discarded for little or no value. Similarly, receivables that accrued prior to the sale also may turn out to be old and uncollectible.

The new owner will also hope that acquiring an existing base of customers and vendors will reduce the time and effort required to establish important business relationships and that it will be possible to take immediate advantage of any existing goodwill toward the products and services of the acquired business. In the same vein, the new owner will generally expect that since the business has a proven track record, it should be easier to secure business financing. While the prior business relationships and record of performance established by the seller are certainly important factors in the buyer's decision to purchase it is ultimately up to the buyer to maintain the same level of service and quality and convince customers, vendors, and lenders that they can be comfortable doing business with the firm after the ownership change has been finalized.

While the buyer should, of course, make a full and thorough investigation of the business before the purchase and sale is completed, it is generally impossible to identify all the potential problems with the target, some of which may not come to light until after the deal is over. For example, buying an operating business means inheriting relationships with existing managers and employees. The new owner may discover that his or her personality clashes with these persons, leading to the possibility of excessive turnover in the important transition months after the sale is completed.

Founder's Dilemmas

Even when armed with the most promising business idea, founders inevitably face a number of challenges from the moment they begin to consider whether or not to form a new company. Wasserman argued that founders must confront a number of "founder's dilemmas" (see Table 3.3) that require difficult decisions with respect to relationships, roles, and rewards and must also honestly assess their own goals and motivations for launching the company and make sure that the choices they make along the way remain aligned with those goals.[13] Based on extensive research into decisions made by founders at the earliest stages of their new ventures Wasserman came up with the following observations and recommendations to guide founders through the process of deciding whether to launch a startup, forming a founding group, allocating duties and responsibilities, establishing reward systems, and bringing on the human resources and investors necessary to stabilize and grow the business:

- The first question for a prospective founder is whether or not it's the right time in his or her career to launch a startup. The founder needs to be sure that he or she has the necessary passion and experience and that the market is ready to be receptive to the proposed product or service.
- In addition to passion the founder needs to critically evaluate whether he or she has the requisite human, social, and financial capital to successfully launch the business without the help of others. In order to "go it alone" a founder must be confident that he or she has expertise in multiple business and technical areas, sufficient capital to get through the startup

---

[13] The discussion of Wasserman's observations and recommendations in this section is based on material appearing in Wasserman, N. 2012. *The Founder's Dilemmas: Anticipating and Avoiding the Pitfalls That Can Sink a Startup.* Princeton, NJ: Princeton University Press.

Table 3.3 Wasserman's founder's dilemmas

- At what point in my career should I consider launching a startup?
- Do I have requisite passion for my idea and the necessary career experience to effectively launch and guide a new business?
- Are there any issues with my personal situation that may prevent me from fearlessly pursuing the new opportunity such as a lack of support from family or insufficient personal financing resources?
- Is the market ready for and receptive to my business idea?
- Should I launch the new business on my own or should I recruit cofounders?
- If cofounders are needed how can I go about identifying appropriate candidates (e.g., friends, family, acquaintances, current or former coworkers, former classmates, or strangers)?
- What positions and responsibilities should each of the cofounders assume in the startup?
- How should decisions be made among the members of the founding group (i.e., what decisions can be made along by one of the founders and which require consultation and how should the consultation and voting be conducted)?
- How should equity and other financial rewards be allocated among the members of the founding group and what provisions should be made for vesting and repurchase of equity upon departure?
- What types of human resources will be required at different stages of the company's growth?
- What special challenges will need to be taken into account for early hires and should they be treated differently than managers and employees hired later in the development of the company?
- What types of investors should be approached at different stages in the development of the company and what challenges will be created for the founder group by introducing outside investors?
- If I am to be the CEO of the company how do I feel about the possibility of being replaced as CEO by a "professional CEO" at some point in the future if required by investors or other stakeholders?

Note: The questions above are adapted from N. Wasserman, *The Founder's Dilemmas: Anticipating and Avoiding the Pitfalls That Can Sink a Startup* (Princeton, NJ: Princeton University Press, 2012), p. 8.

stage and strong connections in the relevant marketplace. If any of these elements are lacking it may be necessary to seek out cofounders who can fill in the gaps.

- When looking for additional founders make a conscious effort to achieve diversity in terms of background, age, experience, and network connections. This not only broadens the collective skill sets of the founding group but also reduces the risk that the founders will run into conflicts when setting their roles and responsibilities. Wasserman cautioned against turning to family and close friends, even if they have the right skills and share the same passion for the ideas and business model, and noted that research confirmed that mixing business with family and friendship too often led to conflict, tension, and bad outcomes for both the company and the relationships.

- Make sure that each of the members of the founding team are clear about expectations with regard to their roles, responsibilities, and contributions and make sure there is an "exit plan" in place that clearly lays out the process for the departure of any of the founders before a problems arises. It is difficult to talk about "breaking up" before a relationship has really begun; however, the founders need to do it, preferably with input from experienced and independent outside advisors who can raise all the questions that the founders may be reluctant to ask.

- Once the founding team has been formed the next step is to assign roles and responsibilities. While the founders may have roughly equivalent equity stakes in the new company and share similar passions about the projected products and services one of them will need to take on the role of chief executive officer (CEO). Wasserman recommended that the best candidate is the founder who is most invested in the startup and notes that this may not necessarily be the founder who came up with the original idea upon which the startup is based.

- An effort should be made to create a clear division of labor among the members of the founding group so that all required activities are managed and overlap is reduced. Proper and clear differentiation of tasks facilitates accountability; however, Wasserman warned about inflexibility in assigning and changing roles and counseled that the founders need to strike the proper balance between division of labor on the one hand and tapping into the creativity that comes from collective work and collaboration. Wasserman also cautioned about handing out titles among members of the founding group

and it is important for all titles to be accompanied by a clear
statement of duties and authority and expectations about how
the holder of that title will interact and collaborate with the
holders of other titles.

- Selecting a CEO and assigning each of the founders one
  or more primary areas of responsibility are part of a larger
  process of developing a decision-making process among
  the founding team and the founders need to decide which
  issues will require debate among all of the founders and how
  those debates will ultimately be resolved. Wasserman noted
  that founding teams take a variety of approaches: some
  choose egalitarian systems in which each of the founders has
  an equal say and a unanimous vote is required and others
  prefer a more hierarchical approach. Regardless of which
  method is used it is important for everyone to understand it
  in advance and to make sure that managers and employees
  outside of the founding group are aware of how the founders
  make their decisions. Even if egalitarianism is not the rule
  the founders are well advised to communicate closely about
  decisions, seek inputs from all of the founders, and make
  sure that all of the founders are aware of the substance of
  important decisions.

- Even though a decision-making process is in place the founders need to anticipate the possibility of conflicts, which, if not
  addressed, may ultimately threaten the viability of the entire
  venture. For example, even though the founders have agreed
  that all of them will be heard on every key issue one of the
  founders may begin to feel frustrated and alienated if decisions continue to go against him or her. Similarly, a founder
  given a title that implies primacy in a particular functional
  area, such as marketing, may feel that the other founders are
  encroaching into his or her domain. The founders need to
  have a plan for settling these fundamental disputes, often
  seeking support and guidance on substance and process
  from trusted outside advisors who are independent of the
  founders, and should also continuously assess responsibilities

in key areas such as product development, sales, marketing, and finance.

- Wasserman recommended that the founders should address the touchy subject of rewards, including the allocation of equity, after they have thoroughly discussed the various issues described above with regard to relationships and roles and everyone has a better idea of how committed each founder will be to the venture and the relative value of each founder's projected contribution to the new business. Wasserman noted that one of the most common problems among founder teams is an initial allocation of equal equity shares among all the members only to find out later that one or more of the founders is unable or unwilling to carry his or her weight or that his or her contribution is simply not as valuable as what is being provided by the other founders.

- Founders have different appetites and expectations regarding the rewards associated with their involvement with a startup and those need to be considered. Some founders are more interested in money and seeing the value of their equity stake increased as quickly as possible while others are more concerned about retaining control over the direction of the business and making sure that their voices are heard when decisions are being made. All of this should be taken into account when allocating equity and assigning rights to the equity interests.

- Founders were encouraged to include vesting provisions in the agreements covering the allocation of equity interests and Wasserman noted that vesting should not be construed as an indication of mistrust but simply as a convenient and realistic tool for making sure that expectations are met and that the founders have an objective means for dealing with unanticipated events such as an egregious failure to perform, a good faith dispute among the founders, the unexpected departure of one of the founders due to illness or death, or the demands of outside investors for changes in the leadership group.

- When establishing the reward systems and equity allocations among the founders consideration also needs to be given to what may be needed in the future to fill in gaps in skills of the members of the founding team and build out the business. If the founders know that large blocks of stock will be needed to bring in a more experienced CEO and/or build out a product development team this should be taken into account from the very beginning. In addition, the founders should anticipate dilution of shareholding by equity that will be sold to outside investors.

The observations and recommendations above pertain mostly to the prefounding stage and the process of building and organizing a founding team; however, Wasserman noted that founders need to consider the steps that will have to be taken to find and attract skills and resources that the founding group does not have and which will be needed to grow the business. The first set of dilemmas beyond the founding group were referred to as "hiring dilemmas" and included questions about what types of people should be recruited and hired to assist the founders and how those persons should be managed during the challenging and turbulent immediately following the launch of a new business. Specific issues include establishing the duties and responsibilities of new hires and selecting the most effective way to compensate them in light of the risks involved. A second set of dilemmas will become relevant when the founders need to approach investors to provide capital beyond the financial resources that the founders are themselves able and willing to contribute to the new venture. Different types of investors will be available at various stages of the development of the company and each of them will have their own demands regarding their equity stake in the company and their ability to exert control over the actions of the founders.

Wasserman argued that it is extremely important for each founder to come to grips with what motivates him or her in taking on the rigors of starting up a new business and investing all the time and effort that will be needed in order to make it successful. According to Wasserman, the two main types of motivation for founders are "control" and "wealth." Founders who are primarily motivated by control can be expected to proceed more slowly and cautiously in allowing outsiders to become involved with the company as cofounders, investors, or employees and will seek to guard their ability to maintain control at each stage of the process of developing new products and services, expanding human resources, and tapping into outside capital. On the other hand, wealth-motivated founders are more open to any reasonable strategy for increasing the value of their ownership stake in the company and thus are more likely to aggressively pursue venture capital even at the risk of losing control of the board of directors and support bringing on experienced talent from outside of the original founder group who can accelerate the growth of the company even if that means that the founder's own equity stake will be diluted.

CHAPTER 4

Founder's Preformation Duties and Liabilities

Introduction

A good deal of the planning for a new business occurs before a new legal entity, such as a corporation, has been formed and founders need to understand that even though a legal entity does not exist they still have certain duties and are subject to potential liabilities to one another, to the new entity and to investors and other outsiders. For example, founders and promoters are placed in a fiduciary capacity with regard to the business entity to be formed and to the other founders and promoters of the entity, if any. As fiduciaries, founders and promoters have a duty to disclose to the entity and its other founders and promoters all material facts relating to transactions with or on behalf of the business entity, and are liable to the entity for any secret profits. Founders and promoters may also be liable to investors under federal and state securities laws for a breach of a fiduciary duty, a failure to disclose material facts, or an omission of material facts in the offer and sale of ownership interests in the new entity.

Founders and promoters, like corporate officers and directors, cannot ordinarily be held personally liable for the acts or obligations of their entity. However, they may become liable if they directly authorize or actively participate in wrongful or tortious conduct. Founders may be held liable for contracts they make for the benefit of a business entity to be formed if they personally make them, unless the other party agrees to look solely to the business entity, when formed, for performance. However, founders are not liable for contracts made in the business entity's name and solely on the business entity's credit. It is important that the founders realize that in their dealings with outside parties during the preformation stage they should make it clear to those parties that any contractual relationship that is being discussed would only be effective if and when the entity is formed and that only the entity would be liable to those parties. Unfortunately for the founders however, since most new business entities do not have sufficient capital or credit history to enter into significant contracts or borrow money on their own outside parties will often insist on personal guarantees of the founders that will remain in place until the entity can stand on its own two feet.

Founder's Duties to Current and Former Employers

Many people decide to launch a new venture while they are still working for another entity and will start the planning process described above well before they terminate their existing employment relationship. During their current employment, the founders may have been exposed to the technology of the current employer, its business practices, financial condition, and customers, all of which have competitive value to the current employer and which can be protected from unauthorized misappropriation by the founders for use in their new business. It is also common for prospective entrepreneurs to develop technology that is competitive with or related to the technology developed and sold by his or her current employer, and/or sell to the same customers of the employer. All of these scenarios create various restrictions on the founders that must be borne in mind as they prepare to launch the new business.

Employees owe certain general duties to their employer regardless of whether or not the employee has a specific employment-related contract. The scope of the duty, and its impact on any new venture that the employee intends to pursue, will depend on a variety of things, such as whether the employee is deemed a skilled or unskilled employee. A key employee (e.g., officer or senior manager) of an existing enterprise owes a duty of loyalty to their company that would prevent them from taking actions causing harm to the company while still in the employment relationship. Examples of such harmful actions include activities such as operating a competing business or usurping a business opportunity that has otherwise been offered to the employer. Similar duties also apply to employees with specialized skills, such as engineers, marketing specialists, or sales representatives. On the other hand, unskilled employees who are not working in positions of trust, or otherwise restricted by a written agreement, may generally work on a new business as long they do not do so on their employer's time or use the employer's facilities or resources.

The type of new business is also an important factor in determining whether an employee violates his or her obligations to a current employer. In general, a person may not engage in a competing business while still working for his or her employer; however, an employee may, in the absence of a written restriction in an employment agreement, establish a noncompeting business so long as it does not interfere with the employee's ability to properly discharge his or her obligations in the current position. But, the employee must be careful not to use the employer's resources to conduct the new business and must also limit his or her activities to periods outside of regular working hours. In addition to the restrictions on competition that apply during the employment terms, former employees may also be under contractual restrictions, which are discussed in detail later in this chapter, that continue to apply for some period of time following the termination of his or her employment relationship.

Disclosure of Future Plans

Employees preparing to leave should be honest with their employer. When employees are vague or evasive regarding their future plans, employers become suspicious. An element of mistrust is created and the employer is unlikely to give the benefit of the doubt to the departing employee. The employer will closely scrutinize the employee's actions, especially his or her posttermination business activities. The disadvantage of being honest is that the advance notice gives the employer time to strike first by filing a lawsuit or to immediately terminate the employee when the employee was counting on receiving additional compensation until the termination date. If possible, a former employee should take a long vacation prior to establishing the new business. The longer the time between the departure date and the establishment of the new business, the less likely it is that a claim for misappropriation of trade secrets will prevail. In addition, if possible, the departing employee should do consulting or accept employment with another company for an interim period. Assuming that the

consulting projects or new employment do not directly compete with
the former employer, this supervening event may cut off liability for
trade secret misappropriation. A departing employee should attempt, if
possible, to avoid directly competing with the former employer.

Return of Property

Individuals who terminate their employment to start a company should
not utilize any of the tools or instrumentalities of the former employer
including telephones, computers, manufacturing equipment, or other
items for planning or starting the new company. Use of such items may
give the employer a claim to ownership of the new business or its assets
and generally appears unfair to the employer, which will hurt the former
employee if litigation results.

Often, former employees take with them such things as their rolodex,
engineering notes, sales prospect list, and other items. These items are
often taken innocently under the belief that they were created by the
employee and thus belong to the employee. This can be a fatal mistake
for a departing employee. No matter how innocent or useless the items
appear to be, the departing employee should not take any property of the
former employer. With many employees working from home, there is a
significant temptation to keep files on the employee's home computer
and other items developed at home. Nevertheless, such items should be
returned to the employer.

On the date of the employee's departure, the employee should have a
representative of the company present when the employee cleans out his
or her office. In addition, the employee should prepare an inventory of
the items left in the office, obtain the signature of the employer's representative, and provide a copy to employer's representative who is witnessing
the packing of one's former office. If an inventory is prepared and signed
by a representative of the employer, the former employer will have difficulty making a trade secret misappropriation claim.

Founder's Agreements with Prior Employers

One common, and always challenging, scenario that arises in connection
with launching a new technology-based business is sorting out ownership

and usage rights of ideas that were initially conceived by the founders while they were still working for their ex-employer. Consider, for example, the questions that might confront two colleagues who leave their positions with a company that develops and manufactures a line of basic widget products to form a new company that will specialize in the development and manufacture of more sophisticated widget products to be marketed into niche markets not currently served by their ex-employer. One of the founders was a design engineer at the old company and will head up the initial product development efforts at the new company. The other founder has a marketing background—in fact, he was a senior product manager at the old company—and will be responsible for sales and marketing at the new company with an initial focus on contacting prospective customers. Each of them signed one or more employment-related agreements with their old company that covered not only their compensation and other terms of employment but also certain obligations relating to protection and use of technology and trade secrets and engaging in activities that might compete with the business and operations of their old company.

As noted above, the founders will generally have various common law responsibilities to their current and former employers that will apply regardless of any contracts that may exist regarding employment relationships of the founders. In addition, however, it should not be surprising to find in the United States that the founders have signed several agreements with current and/or former employers, or a single agreement covering all of the areas that might be addressed by separate agreements—an employment agreement; a nondisclosure and assignment of innovations agreement; a noncompetition and/or nonsolicitation agreement; and a stock purchase and/or option agreement. Each agreement raises specific concerns for the new business, and each of the founders on a personal level, which are discussed in the following sections.

Employment Agreements

Employment agreements lay out the mutual understanding of the parties (i.e., the employer and the employee) with respect to the fundamental terms of the employment relationship—duties and reporting requirements; salary, bonuses, and other cash compensation; benefits;

reimbursement of certain expenses; term and termination; and dispute resolution. While all of these issues are important to founders as they reach the point where they want to launch the new company it will be the provisions relating to termination of employment that are most relevant as they consider when to break their ties to their old company and officially launch their new venture. In general, they would have the right to terminate the employment relationship at any time and for any reason; however, senior executives and managers may have conditions in their employment agreements that require them to forfeit certain prospective benefits if they fail to remain employed for a minimum period of time (e.g., forfeiture of unvested stock and options and/or repayment of bonuses). There will be a temptation to continue receiving the salary and other benefits from the old company for as long as possible if financial support for the new venture is not in place; however, this is a risky proposition since engaging in all the activities associated with launching the new venture while still employed by the old company may trigger a right in favor of the old company to terminate the employment agreement "for cause" and seek damages from the employee. Even in cases where the founders are required to provide advance notice of their intent to terminate their employment relationship, they should expect that the employer will ask them to leave immediately and demand strict compliance with any agreements the founders may have made regarding return and protection of confidential information of the employer.

Nondisclosure and Assignment of Innovations Agreements

Many new ventures are built on a foundation of confidential business information or ideas, which, properly applied, provide the enterprise with a competitive advantage. This information can be protected as a "trade secret" so long as it has value to the business owner and is not generally known or readily ascertainable in the industry. Such information also will be protected by the law if the company expends the necessary effort to maintain the secrecy of the information. While most states prohibit the use of trade secrets regardless of whether or not the employee signed an agreement prohibiting use or disclosure, it is common practice to have employees, particularly key employees, sign a nondisclosure or confidentiality agreement to impose contractual obligations on them not to engage in unauthorized uses of the trade secrets and other proprietary information of their employer. In addition, employees engaged in creative activities, particularly the development of new technologies and products that may qualify for protection under patent and other laws recognizing and enforcing proprietary rights (e.g., copyright and trademark laws), will be required to enter into agreements that assign and transfer any rights they may have in these "innovations" to their employer. The scope of the assignment is generally quite broad and includes all inventions conceived, developed, or created by the employee during the course of employment. The assignment requirement typically extends beyond inventions eligible for patent protection to include material that would be covered under the copyright laws while employed by the company. In many ways, such agreements reinforce the employer's common law rights to ownership of inventions conceived by an employee when the employee was "hired to invent." However, they often go further than that and require that the employee assign inventions that are created within a specified period of time, such as one year, after the employee leaves the company.

These agreements create duties that extend beyond termination of employment and may definitely have an impact on what the founders can and cannot do in launching and building their new business. Failure to comply with these agreements may expose the founders, and their new company, to civil liability and possibly criminal penalties; however, the scope of potential liability to a former employer will depend upon what the founders did in their prior job, the generally accepted level of knowledge in the industry, the availability of certain information in the public domain, and the anticipated duties and activities of the founders at the new company.

Regardless of whether there is a specific contract on the matter, employees are not permitted to take tangible or intangible information that is deemed to be "owned" by their employer with them when they leave the employment of the company. Deciding just what is owned by the employer can be a challenge and there is a great deal of uncertainty that may create risks for employees when they are attempting to engage in activities that are similar to those of their ex-employer. The founders would be entitled to take their knowledge and skills with them; however, issues may arise with respect to replicating and using methods, processes and systems that were conceived or otherwise learned while they worked for the ex-employer. The level of scrutiny that the ex-employer may use in monitoring the activities of the founders will depend on their positions and whether or not they had access to particularly sensitive information. Issues in this area are not confined to employees engaged in inventive activities and there may be risks for employees who served in sales and marketing positions and seek to use information that the ex-employer considers to be a trade secret (e.g., customer lists and data base information about customer requirements). Misappropriation claims may be rebutted by showing that the information is publicly available, generally known in the industry and/or voluntarily disclosed to the new company by the customer or other business partner.

Founders who have been employed as scientists or engineers or otherwise directly engaged in research and development activities with their former employers will typically be required to execute an assignment of innovations agreement. The scope of the assignment is subject to specific limitations and restrictions that may be imposed by applicable state laws (e.g., it must be shown that the employee used equipment and tools provided by the employer and conceived the invention or innovation during the time that he was obligated to perform duties on behalf of the employer); however, the effect of the assignment is to preclude the employee from freely using the invention or other innovation in his or her future business activities even if the ex-employer is not actively exploiting the invention or innovation. If the founders intend to build their new business on improvements and enhancements to technology developed at their ex-employer they should consult experienced patent counsel to determine whether the anticipated improvements and enhancements will fall within the scope of the ownership rights of the prior employer. If an actual or potential conflict arises the new business may be badly crippled from the start if the former employer asserts an infringement claim and/or demands that the new business obtain a license to use the technology that the founders worked on while employed by the ex-employer.

Noncompetition and Nonsolicitation Agreements

Many employees, particularly executives and mid-level managers, may be required to enter into covenants with their employer that restrict their ability to engage in competitive activities and/or solicit customers, employees, and other business partners of their employer during and after their term of employment. The existence of a non-competition agreement can be a significant problem for the founders if they intend to engage in business activities that are similar to those of their ex-employer even if they reasonably believe that the new business will not harm or impact the ex-employer. Nonsolicitation agreements can be problematic when the founders approach customers of their ex-employer or consider staffing their new venture with qualified colleagues that they worked with at their ex-employer. One of the most valuable assets of any business is the pool of employees who understand the company and how it works. As such, it is not surprising that restrictions are placed on attempts by a departing employee to actively encourage other employees to join the new company and many contracts actually prohibit the hiring of any other employees of the old company for a certain period of time after the departing employee leaves regardless of whether there has been active solicitation.

While such covenants are common, they will only be enforceable if they satisfy certain strict requirements and in the United States, the enforceability of noncompetition agreements varies widely from state to state. In most cases, the contract must be designed to protect the legitimate interests of the employer, be limited in scope, and not be contrary to the public interest. However, some states frown upon such agreements as inappropriate restrictions on the ability of employees to freely pursue their livelihood. In California, for example, such agreements are generally unenforceable on public policy grounds although there are some limited exceptions to the general rule of unenforceability that may apply and employees are certainly precluded from using the trade secrets of a former employer to compete with it.

When forming a new company founders often underestimate the importance of all these issues or naively assume that their ex-employer will not be concerned because the new company will be developing products or seeking entry into markets that were not of current interest to the ex-employer. In fact, one reason that talented scientists and engineers leave larger companies is because they are frustrated that their senior managers are not willing to invest resources in the opportunities that they are planning to pursue with their new company. However, even if the ex-employer is not active in the area of focus of the new company the founders must nonetheless expect that the ex-employer will want to protect its intellectual property rights and either seek compensation from the founders for the right to use its patents and other technology or preserve the option to sell or license those rights to other parties that the ex-employer considers to be better situated to create value from exploitation of the rights. Even if the new venture does not create issues of intellectual property ownership the founders may be deemed to have fiduciary duties to their ex-employer not to divert business opportunities that came to them as a result of their employment with their prior company.

Stock Purchase and Option Agreements

Employees may have purchased shares of their ex-employer and/or received options to purchase such shares. Upon termination of their employment with their ex-employer the founders must consider how the event will impact their rights with respect to such shares or options. It is common for companies to impose "vesting" conditions that are intended to ensure that employees remain employed by the company for a specified minimum period of time before they obtain full and nonforfeitable ownership rights over their equity interests in the company. For example, an employee may be allowed to purchase 10,000 common shares; however, the acquisition of the shares may be subject to vesting restrictions that allow the company to repurchase all or a portion of such shares at the price paid by the employee if the employment relationship terminates before a specified date. Typically these repurchase rights partially lapse as the employee satisfies certain milestones with respect to his or her tenure with the company. In the case of the example above the repurchase right may continue for four years, but the percentage of the shares that the company may repurchase may decrease by 25 percent on each annual anniversary of the original purchase of the shares. The right to exercise an option may also be subject to vesting requirements and options to purchase shares that have vested prior to termination of employment usually must be exercised within a short period of time following termination or will be deemed to have been forfeited.

CHAPTER 5

Founder's Relationships and Agreements

Fundamental Questions Regarding Founder's Relations

As discussed later in this chapter, one of issues that the founders need to consider is the form of legal entity for operation of their new business venture (e.g., corporation, partnership, or limited liability company); however, regardless of the form of entity selected the founders need to sit down and carefully discuss the relationship that will exist among the founders with respect to ownership and management of the business before outside investors are brought into the picture. When properly done, the ownership structure will protect the rights of each founder while creating incentives to make the business grow well into the future. The structure should always be flexible enough to adapt to future changes, including new employees and capital-raising from outside investors. Among the questions that need to be asked are the following:

- What percentage of the company will be owned by each founder?
- What rights will each of the founders have with respect to the management and control of the company?
- What tangible contributions (e.g., money, property, contract rights, etc.) will each founder make to the company and how will they be valued?
- How much time will each founder be expected to devote to the business?
- What incentives will be used to motivate each of the founders to remain actively involved with the business of the company?

- What procedures should be followed when a founder dies, becomes disabled, reaches retirement age, or voluntarily leaves the company prior to retirement age?
- What procedures should be followed to expel a founder from the company?
- Are there other persons outside the founding group who are likely to become actively involved in the business of the company?

The founders may be more interested in spending time on developing their new products and services than on dealing with what can often be very difficult and divisive issues. However, if these questions are not addressed at the beginning of the venture, it is likely that trouble will erupt down the road.

Allocation of Ownership Interests

In general, ownership determines how profits from the business will be shared and management rights will be exercised. Each form of business entity can be adapted so that certain founders enjoy greater economic rights as opposed to voting rights and vice-versa. In dividing ownership, consideration should be given to all of the actual and potential contributions of the founders to the business. For example, the founders may ascribe value to any or all of the following: cash and property contributed by the founders at the time that the new business is launched, including the costs to the founders of acquiring or developing the property; the value of anticipated future contributions by the founders, including cash, property, services, business development assistance, and introductions to business partners; and the opportunity costs to the founders of launching the new business. Obviously, it is difficult to value several of these factors, particularly those which are speculative and depend on performance in the future. However, it is important for each founder to believe that his or her contributions have been fairly recognized. Professional advisors working with the founders of an emerging company will likely recommend that weight or credit should be given to discovery or conception of the ideas underlying the business; the time and effort expended in leading and managing efforts to promote those ideas; the level of financial and personal risk assumed in forming and launching the business; the amount of income foregone by forming the company and accepting a nominal or modest salary during the initial development period; the amount of effort spent in writing a formal business plan for the company; the specialized expertise contributed toward the development of new technology and/or products; and the background, training, and experience that the founder expects to bring to crucial postformation activities associated with the actual commercialization of the company's technology or products.

In some cases, one of the founders of a new business may contribute intangible property and services while the other founders are providing the cash necessary to fund the development and marketing of the products based on the intangibles. Since the founders may reasonably differ as to the value to be placed on the contributions of the noncash participant, counsel must proceed carefully to make sure that the assets are fairly valued. In that situation, counsel is faced with reconciling the following issues:

- What method(s) should be used to value the intangible property and services be valued for purposes of determining the relative equity ownership of the business?
- What obligations, if any, will be imposed on the parties to make additional capital contributions?
- Who will own the rights to trade secrets, patentable, or copyrightable information? Will the founder retain ownership and license them to the entity, or will the entity own all the rights?
- What obligations will be imposed on the "inventor" with respect to continued development of the intangible property?
- Who will own the rights to the intangible property in the event the company merges or dissolves?

Another issue to keep in mind is the possibility that the relative ownership interests of the founders will be diluted by future events, such as the need to grant an ownership interest to new managers, key employees, and one or more groups of outside investors. For example, a founding group looking for venture capital funding may discover that they will need to set aside 5–10 percent of the equity for filling out the management team, 10–20 percent of the equity for a pool of incentives for new employees, and 40–60 percent of the equity for sale to the venture capitalists.

Transfer Restrictions

It is typical for the founders to enter into various agreements that impose restrictions on their ability to free transfer ownership interests in the business. First of all, vesting restrictions may be used to ensure that the founders remain with the company long enough to provide the anticipated value that was implicit in their ownership interest. If an owner should leave the company before an interest has vested, the company and/ or the other owners would have the right to acquire the ownership interest on favorable terms (e.g., at cost payable in installments over a period of time). Once a founder's rights in his or her ownership interest have vested, other restrictions would apply that limit the disbursement of control outside the original founder group while at the same time providing the founders with some opportunity to gain liquidity for their interests in the event they become dissociated with the company.

- A right of first refusal provides the company and/or the owners with the first opportunity to purchase ownership interests that the founder wishes to sell to a third party. Such a provision can prevent the sale of ownership interests to outsiders and generally will substantially limit the transferability of the interests.
- A buy–sell agreement restricts transfers of ownership interests by granting the company and/or the other owners the right to purchase the interest of an owner upon the occurrence of certain events, such as a proposed sale of the ownership interest to a third party, death or disability of the owner, termination of employment, bankruptcy, or divorce. Buy–sell agreements may also provide liquidity by requiring that the company and/or the other owners purchase the interest of the deceased or disabled owner. Procedures for determining the value of an

interest upon any required purchase and sale will be included in the agreement.

- Co-sale agreements, which are often used when venture capitalists invest in the company, allow outside investors to sell their ownership interests at the same time that the founders sell their interests. A co-sale right often is coupled with a right of first refusal and thus allows the investors to choose between purchasing the founder's interests or selling out on the same terms and conditions.

Management of the New Business

Regardless of the consideration they provide for their ownership interests, the founders must consider potentially contentious matters relating to control of the business. For example, decisions must be made regarding the voting rights of each of the founders and their power to control membership of the board of directors or other management body. The key issues to be considered include the following:

- What voice will each founder have in the election of the members of the managing body, such as the board of directors?
- Who will be responsible for the day-to-day operations of the business (e.g., officers of the corporation)?
- What level of consensus among the founding group will be required for major transaction, such as sale or merger of the company, major debt financings, and issuances of securities?
- What are to be the terms of any employment agreements between the company and the founders, including the amount of salary and other benefits to be paid to owners who are to be active in the business?
- What procedures should be used to resolve any disputes among the members of the founding group?
- How are the members of the founding group going to participate in the profits generated by the business?

- What restrictions should be placed on the outside activities of the founder, as well as their ability to transfer their ownership interests in the company?

The founders will often turn to an attorney to assist them in considering these issues and documenting their decisions. The legal counsel needs to be aware that the negotiation and drafting of an owner's agreement will often lead to conflicts of interest such that the attorney cannot represent the founders concurrently. Even if all sides are properly informed of potential conflicts and grant the appropriate waivers, counsel still walks a fine line since it may be impossible to anticipate all the conflicts that might ultimately arise in the future. Accordingly, the attorney should be ready to prepare some form of disclosure letter and obtain a waiver of potential conflicts from each of the founders. If the founders are unwilling to waive the conflicts, separate counsel should be retained.

The members of the founding group should enter into an agreement among themselves as to how the company will be operated. In the corporate context, such an agreement is generally referred to as a pre-incorporation or shareholder's agreement. In the case of a partnership or an LLC, the matters are typically covered in a separate part of the partnership agreement or operating agreement, respectively. In some cases, the founders will address these issues before the entity is formed in some type of preformation agreement. This can be a useful exercise since it can give the founders a good idea of whether they will be able to live and work with each other before they incur the additional expense of actually forming the entity. Voting agreements are often used to establish procedures for making decisions regarding important matters relating to the business. In the case of a corporation, voting procedures may be laid out in a separate shareholder's or voting agreement. Voting provisions for partnership and limited liability companies are set out in the partnership or operating agreement, respectively. The founders may elect to cover a variety of matters in the voting agreement, including the vote required to elect the managers of the company and approve fundamental changes in the business, including a sale of the company or its assets, significant borrowings, and admission of new owners. Transactions between the company and one of the owners may also be subject to special approval procedures.

Whenever an owner's agreement is implemented, an evidence of an ownership interest (e.g., a share certificate) should include a legend that notifies third parties of the existence of a restriction on the rights of the owners with respect to transfers or exercise of economic or control rights.

Employment Agreements

Some or all of the members of the founding group may also enter into employment agreements with the company that describe their duties and responsibilities with the company, the terms of compensation for their services and, perhaps most importantly, the rights and obligations of the company and the founder upon termination of the founder's employment relationship with the company. Employment agreements are often valuable to founders who hold a minority ownership interest in the equity of the company and who seek protection against the possibility that they will be discharged by some concerted action of the majority owners. In addition, however, employment agreements can serve a number of purposes beyond merely providing protection to minority owners and setting forth the terms of compensation. Employment agreements that contain noncompetition provisions serve to protect the other founder in the event that the employee-founder leaves the enterprise and attempts to start a competing business. The employment agreement also settles issues regarding the ownership and use of intellectual property rights acquired by the entity.

Shareholder's Agreements

The answers to the fundamental questions regarding founder's relations discussed above will normally provide the basis for drafting various contractual agreements among the founders in their roles as shareholders with respect to corporate governance and their duties and responsibilities to the corporation and one another. These "shareholders agreements," which complement and supplement the provisions in the articles of incorporation and bylaws that will generally govern the operation and management of the corporation, can include an "agreement to incorporation," which is actually entered into before the corporation is formally formed and organized; voting agreements; and buy–sell agreements. In some cases, the founders may opt for a comprehensive shareholder's agreement, which covers a wide array of governance issues beyond the election of directors, including designation of officers; voting requirements for fundamental corporate changes, such as mergers, the sale of all of the corporate assets and the issuance of a significant number of new shares; dividend policies; and alternative dispute resolution procedures. In addition to governance issues, a "hybrid" shareholder's agreement often covers issues normally addressed in stock purchase agreements, employment agreements, intellectual property agreements, noncompetition agreements, and buy–sell agreements. Finally, founders wishing to create a detailed set of guidelines regarding management and operation of the corporation may include provisions relating to investment of corporate funds, maintenance of books and records, indemnification of directors and officers, and inspection and auditing of corporate records. See Table 5.1 for a comprehensive list of questions to consider during the negotiation and drafting of an agreement among the owners of a new corporation.

Table 5.1 Matters to consider in drafting an agreement to incorporate

1. Names and addresses of the parties
2. The proposed name of the corporation and a description of the procedures that will be followed to check the availability of the name and reserve it for future use on behalf of the corporation
3. A description of the proposed purpose and activities of the corporation
4. A summary of the place or places where it is anticipated that the corporation will conduct its business, including a statement of the procedures that will be followed in order to qualify the corporation as a foreign corporation
5. A description of the proposed capitalization of the corporation, including subscriptions by the parties
6. A list of the incorporators, initial directors, and officers of the corporation
7. A description of the terms of engagement of any persons required to assist in the incorporation process, such as lawyer, accountants, or appraisers
8. A description of the terms of any proposed employment relationship between the new corporation and any of its organizers and/or promoters
9. The general terms of any buy–sell arrangements among the corporation and its future shareholders
10. If the principals wish to have the corporation treated as a Subchapter S corporation for tax purposes, the agreement may contain various covenants regarding the steps that will be taken to perfect and maintain Subchapter S status

11. A description of any proposed purchase of assets by the new corporation, which will be relevant whenever the new corporation is going to take over the operations of a going concern
12. When subscriptions will be sought from persons not otherwise affiliated with the founding group, a description of the procedures that will be followed in making the offering, including the preparation of an offering document, engagement of investment bankers, and payment of the fees and expenses associated with complying with any securities law requirements
13. If an existing business will be incorporated, a description of the assets that will be transferred to the new corporation, the shares that will be issued in exchange for each proprietor's interest and a summary of the tax elections that will be made in connection with the incorporation

Agreements to Form a New Corporation

An agreement to form a new corporation, sometimes called an "agreement to incorporate," should be considered as a valuable opportunity to reduce to writing the understanding of the founders regarding the general terms and conditions associated with the formation and initial organization of the new corporation (see Table 5.2). The content of an agreement to incorporate will vary depending upon the circumstances; however, the matters commonly covered in such an agreement include the names and addresses of the parties; the proposed name of the corporation and a description of the procedures that will be followed to check the availability of the name and reserve it for future use on behalf of the corporation; a description of the proposed purpose and activities of the corporation; a summary of the place or places where it is anticipated that the corporation will conduct its business, including a statement of the procedures that will be followed in order to qualify the corporation as a foreign corporation; a description of the proposed capitalization of the corporation, including subscriptions by the founders; a list of the incorporators, initial directors, and officers of the corporation; and a description of the terms of engagement of any persons required to assist in the incorporation process, such as lawyers, accountants, or appraisers.

Other matters that might be covered in an agreement to incorporate are listed in Table 5.2 and include a description of the terms of any proposed employment relationship between the new corporation and any of the founders; the general terms of any share transfer restrictions and/or buy–sell arrangements among the corporation and its future shareholders;

Table 5.2 *Questions for preparation of owner's agreement*

Background

- What general subjects should be covered by the terms of the agreement? Consider regulation of future issuances of ownership interests; management and control of the business; establishment of employment relationships; and buy–sell arrangements.
- What is the term of the agreement? Consider having the agreement remain in effect for a fixed term or until terminated by a vote of all or a specified percentage-in-interest of the parties.
- What procedures should be included for amendment or modification of the agreement (e.g., vote or consent of all parties)?

Ownership Interests

- What percentage of the ownership interests will be held by each founder? Will it be necessary to commission a valuation of non-cash assets which the founders might contribute to the business?
- Should the agreement provide for preemptive rights for the founders with respect to future issuances of ownership interests?

Management and Control

- What procedures should be included for insuring that the founders will cooperate regarding the election of the managers of the business? Issues to be considered include the number of persons serving on the managing board of the entity; persons to be elected as members of the managing board; functions of managing board; resolution of disputes among members of the managing board; persons to be elected as officers (including titles); and manager's and owner's meetings. A detailed description of officer's duties may also be included.
- What instructions should be included regarding protection and disbursements of the fund of the business? Consider language regarding location of bank accounts and signature requirements for checks.
- How will the founders select accountants and auditors for the business? What financial reports should be prepared for the owners?
- What matters should require the consent of all the founders? Consider issuances of additional ownership interests; sales of significant assets; execution of contracts that impose material financial obligations from the business; significant increases in salaries; mergers and consolidations; and/or changes in the business of the entity.
- Should the agreement include provisions regarding the payment of dividends or other distributions of profits? Consider either allowing the directors to determine the timing of dividends or requiring payment of some minimum dividend amount (subject to any restrictions on dividends or distributions included in applicable state law).
- What books and records should be maintained by the business? Note the need to comply with minimum requirements established by applicable statutes and related regulations.

Employment Matters

- Should the agreement include provisions relating to employment of the founders by the business? If so, consider the following issues: duties of each founder in his or her capacity as an employee and the amount of time that each founder will spend on the activities of the business; the amount of compensation to be paid to each employee-founder (including benefits); and the circumstances under which employment of a founder may be terminated.

- Should the agreement include restrictions on the ability of the founders to engage in competitive activities?
- Should the entity be required to purchase health and/or life insurance and/or disability insurance with respect to any of the founders?
- What types of obligations should be imposed on the founders regarding protection of the confidential information of the business? A definition of confidential information should be included in the text of the agreement. The agreement should also provide for assignment of the founder's business-related inventions to the entity.

Buy–Sell Provisions

- Should the agreement include restrictions on transfers of ownership interests? In many cases, the transfer of interests may be subject to a right of first offer or refusal in favor of the entity and/or the other owners. Transfers should be broadly defined to include all possible voluntary and involuntary means of transfer including gift, pledge, hypothecation, operation of law (e.g., dissolution of marriage), and intestate succession. Restriction should apply to the founders, personal representatives of deceased or incompetent founders, founder's spouses, and permitted transferees.
- Should the agreement grant one or more of the founders the right to compel the entity to purchase the interests of other specified founders? Such a provision may be helpful in the case of a deadlock among the ownership group.
- Should the agreement provide for optional or mandatory purchase of ownership interests upon disability of a founder? If so, how should disability be defined?
- Should the agreement provide for optional or mandatory purchase of ownership interests upon the termination of employment of a founder? If so, what events should constitute termination of employment?
- Should the agreement provide for mandatory purchase of the ownership interests of a deceased founder?
- Should the agreement provide for optional or mandatory purchase of ownership interests which become subject to transfer to a third party in an involuntary transfer (e.g., a transfer pursuant to a judicial order or enforcement of pledge)?
- How is the purchase price for ownership interests subject to buy–sell provisions to be determined? For example, the parties may agree that the value of the interests will be the sum of the book value of the interests as reflected in the financial statements of the entity plus an amount equal to the value of the goodwill associated with the interests. The price may vary depending on the event that triggers the buy–sell provision, such as when interests subject to involuntary transfers are purchased at the lower of the price determined pursuant to the above formula or the price actually paid by the third party for the interests.
- What provisions should be included for payment of the purchase price for ownership interests bought and sold under the buy–sell agreement? For example, a portion of the price may be paid immediately in cash and the balance may be paid out in installment payments under a promissory note. Consider the need to purchase insurance to finance purchases.

Note: In the case of a corporation, the owner's agreement would take the form of a shareholder's agreement that would cover a variety of matters, including the allocation of ownership interests, voting rights, and restrictions on transfers of shares. In the case of a partnership or limited liability company, the provisions might be incorporated into the partnership or operating agreement, respectively. Regardless of the form of documentation used, it is important for the founders to consider all of the issues raised above before proceeding with the actual formation of the new entity.

a description of any proposed purchase of assets by the new corporation, which will be relevant whenever the new corporation is going to take over the operations of a going concern; and a description of the procedures that will be followed in offering shares to persons not otherwise affiliated with the founding group, including the preparation of an offering document, engagement of finders, and payment of the fees and expenses associated with complying with any securities law requirements.

The agreement to incorporate is also the place to address specific tax and regulatory issues associated with the formation and operation of the new corporation. For example, if the new corporation is being formed in the United States and the founders wish to have it treated as a Subchapter S corporation for federal income tax purposes, the agreement should contain various covenants regarding the steps that will be taken to perfect and maintain Subchapter S status. In the case of regulated businesses it will be necessary to ensure that the corporation can obtain the appropriate license or permit. Compliance with securities laws should also be addressed if shares will be offered to outside parties. Finally, if an existing legal entity, such as a partnership, is being converted to a corporation, agreement should be reached on the assets that will be transferred to the new corporation and the number of shares that the owners of the old entity will receive in exchange and attention must be paid to ensuring that they achieve the tax treatment they are expecting with respect to the conversion.

Shareholder's Voting Arrangements

Probably the most common reason for entering into a shareholder's agreement is to set out the terms of any special arrangements among the founders regarding voting of their shares once they become shareholders. The power to elect the members of the board of directors of a corporation is held by the shareholders, and the power to elect all or a majority of the directors is held by those shareholders who own a majority of the outstanding stock of the corporation. Under certain circumstances, however, the shareholders may wish to allocate voting rights in some manner other than based on the ownership of shares. For example, a special arrangement might be used when all of the shareholders in a closely held corporation want to ensure they will serve on the board of directors. Another situation is when a shareholder wishes to reduce his or her ownership interest in the corporation for estate planning purposes while retaining the voting control, at least while the shareholder remains actively involved in the management of the business. Finally, a minority shareholder may be unwilling to invest needed capital without assurances that he or she will have some ability to participate on the board.

Voting arrangements may take a variety of forms, including voting trusts, irrevocable proxies, and voting or "pooling" agreements. Under a voting trust, which is authorized by statute, one or more shareholders transfer record title to their shares to designated individuals who act as voting trustees in accordance with the terms of the voting trust agreement entered into by the participating shareholders, which terms include directions as to how shares held in the trust will be voted. Voting trusts can operate as an easy and self-executing means for ensuring that the votes are cast in the manner specified. However, voting trusts can be somewhat costly to create and maintain; although simplified versions of such an agreement can be drafted to meet the needs of closely held corporations. When using a voting trust reference must be made to the guidelines included in the applicable state corporation laws. An irrevocable proxy is an arrangement whereby one or more shareholders irrevocably grant to another person or persons, who need not be shareholders, the right to vote the shares owned by the granting shareholders for the duration and to the extent described in the proxy. Certain statutory procedures must be followed in order to ensure that a proxy is irrevocable.

Voting arrangements may be used with, or in lieu of, other mechanisms for allocating control over a corporation. For example, different shareholder groups may be provided with the ability to elect directors by issuing various classes of stock. Similarly, issuing one class of stock with full voting rights and another class of stock with no voting rights can have the same effect as a contractual voting arrangement. Of course, voting arrangements are not self-executing, and the existence of a voting arrangement does not mean that the corporation must dispense with the legal formalities of shareholder action, such as meetings or actions by written consent.

Voting or Pooling Agreements

A voting agreement, which is often referred to as a "pooling" agreement, is often entered into by two or more shareholders to provide for the manner in which each of them will vote their shares. Voting agreements are authorized by statute and specifically enforceable. A voting agreement is often preferred over voting trusts and irrevocable proxies because it can be specifically tailored to the needs of the parties. For example, a voting agreement might be limited to votes taken for the election of directors, leaving the parties free to vote their shares as they see fit on any other matters. Voting agreements are also much easier to implement than voting trusts.

A voting agreement may provide that shares will be voted to elect specified directors or voted in the manner directed by a majority of the members of the pool. For example, the shareholders of a closely held corporation might agree to elect one another to the board of directors under a voting agreement. Another situation where a voting agreement may be used is when the founders of a corporation seek to guarantee control over the composition of the board by requiring other holders of common stock, particularly employees, to become parties to a voting agreement that grants the founders the right to vote the shares of the employees for the nominees chosen by the founders. This allows the founders to create economic incentives and rewards for the employees based on success of the business, and appreciation of the value of their common shares, while retaining control over management and the composition of the board.

Voting agreements may continue as they are not limited in duration, unlike voting trusts, and thus may continue indefinitely. If new parties are to be added to a voting agreement, provision should be made for use of a formal accession agreement that includes a specific acknowledgment by the new party that he, she, or it must be bound by the agreement. Title to the shares subject to the pooling agreement remains in the shareholders who are parties to the agreement and this means, of course, that the agreement is not self-executing. Each party is obligated to vote his or her shares as provided for in the agreement, but a vote breaching the agreement is not void and in the case of a breach the other parties must bring an action seeking specific performance or damages.

Shareholder's agreements relating to corporate governance should be drafted in light of the resolution of broader issues relating to management and control of the corporation. Close corporation statutes, and general business corporation statutes in a few states, permit the shareholders to enter agreements to substantially reduce the powers of, or even eliminate, the board, and vest control of the corporation directly in the shareholders. If the board is eliminated, the shareholders will still provide for the election of officers to manage the day-to-day affairs of the corporation. If the board is retained, consideration should be given to having the shareholder's agreement address the election of directors and supermajority shareholder quorum and voting requirements. For example, the parties to a shareholder's agreement sometimes provide for supermajority requirements at the board level, which require consensus among the directors and generally protect minority shareholders, or restrictions on the discretion and powers of directors and officers which force more decisions back up to the shareholder level.

Shareholder's Agreements and Election of Directors

As a general rule, shareholders voting in the election of directors will follow the principles of "one-share–one-vote," unless some other provision as to the election of directors is included in the articles and bylaws or in a separate shareholder's agreement. Some, but not all, states automatically provide for cumulative voting in the election of directors, thereby assuring that holders of less than a majority of the voting shares will be able to elect some representatives to the board of directors. In other states, cumulative voting with respect to the election of directors is only available if it is actually provided for in the articles.

A voting agreement may be used to deviate from the "one-share–one-vote" rule by providing that the parties will pool their shares to elect directors in accordance with the terms of the agreement. In addition to the examples discussed above, these types of provisions may be used in situations where the shareholder group consists of both founders and employees on the one hand and outside investors on the other hand. For example, the parties may provide that the outside investors will initially have the right to designate a specified number of directors and that the remaining directors will be designated by the founders and other members of the management group. Another option is for the investors and management to be given the right to designate an equal number of directors and require that the remaining director or directors must be agreed upon by both groups of shareholders.

In deciding whether to utilize one of the alternative procedures for the election of directors, consideration must be given to the objectives of the investors, the relationship that exists between the investors and the founders and other members of the management group, and the anticipated future financing requirements of the company. For example, in situations where the investors are purchasing a majority interest in the company, they may, as a result of the operation of statutory voting provision, have the right to elect all of the directors. However, recognizing that it is probably desirable to take a balanced approach to board representation, the investors may agree to an alternative voting scheme, which assures them of the right to retain control of the board while allowing one or more members of management to also serve as directors. In any case, the procedures regarding representation on the board will always be heatedly negotiated when the company raises additional funds in future equity financings.

If the investors are not initially given the right to designate a majority of the directors, they may bargain for ability to assume control of the board upon the occurrence of certain events specified in the agreement. The triggers for these "vote switch" provisions, which are referred to by that name since they effectively switch control over the company's affairs from the management group to the investors, are always the subject of intense negotiations. In some cases, changes in control may be limited to situations in which the company fails to make a required redemption, defaults its obligations to make a dividend payment, or becomes involved in insolvency or bankruptcy proceedings. However, the parties may specify additional events, including a default by the company under any covenants made to the investors or the company's failure to satisfy specific financial tests.

Supermajority Shareholder Quorum and Voting Requirements

The matters normally requiring shareholder approval, and the vote required to approve such matters, are set out in the applicable state corporation statutes. While many matters concerning the operations for the corporation can be dealt with by majority rule, there are generally some actions that should not be taken by a closely held corporation without obtaining the consent of all of the shareholders, or some percentage-in-interest of the shares that is well in excess of a simple majority vote. These "supermajority" voting requirements are often covered in the articles and bylaws; however, they are also a proper topic for shareholder's agreements. It is important not to unnecessarily bog down day-to-day activities by requiring that every decision be placed in front of all of the shareholders but it is not uncommon to require "supermajority" approval of operating plans and budgets; issuances of additional shares; sales of significant assets of the corporation; execution of contracts that impose material financial obligations from the corporation; significant increases in salaries; mergers and consolidations; changes in the business of the corporation; and activities that specifically contradict the terms of the shareholder's agreement. Supermajority shareholder quorum and voting requirements are often used as a means for protecting the interests of minority shareholders. There are, of course, other strategies that can be used to achieve a fair result for all parties without running the risk of a deadlock due to a minority shareholder unreasonably withholding his or her consent. For example, minority shareholders may be convinced to allow the used "majority rule" to apply to a proposed sale of the company provided that the transaction yields all shareholders at least a specified minimum amount per share.

Dispute Resolution Procedures

A shareholder's agreement is a great place to set out procedures for resolving disputes among the shareholders in a manner that avoids a forced dissolution of the corporation. For example, it is not uncommon for the agreement to provide that in the event that the board is unable to reach a decision on any matter an independent "provisional director" will be designated who will serve solely for the purpose of resolving the particular dispute. If a provisional director procedure is used, the parties should agree to indemnify the designee for acts taken while serving as a director.

Arbitration clauses may also be included in the shareholder's agreement. Arbitration is ordinarily quicker and cheaper than litigation and may be an efficient solution to dissension and deadlock. In addition, it is more flexible than litigation in dealing with the complex problems encountered by the close corporation and in devising remedies for those problems. If other means of resolving the conflict fail, the shareholder's agreement might include a "put" or "call" in favor of one or more of the shareholders, which will allow for an orderly withdrawal of members of the shareholder group without dissolving the corporation and disrupting the business. However, any such provision must be carefully drafted and used in a way that does not amount to a violation of the fiduciary obligations of the controlling shareholders.

Buy–Sell Agreements

A buy–sell agreement is strongly recommended for clients involved in establishing and operating a closely held business, regardless of whether the business is operated as a corporation, partnership, or limited liability company. The subject matter of a buy–sell agreement can usefully be broken down into two areas: transfer restrictions and buy–sell provisions. While ownership interests in business entities, such as the shares of a corporation, are considered to be personal property over which the owner has the absolute right to sell and transfer, there are a number of reasons why the owners of a closely held business are generally willing to accept various restrictions on transfers of such interests, such as in the following cases:

- The owners want retain the power to choose their future associates and co-workers.
- The owners want to prevent the business from falling under the control of competitors.
- The owners wish to ensure that all of them are actively involved in the business and avoid conflicts that may arise between active and passive investors.
- Restrictions are required in order to comply with federal and state securities laws.
- The owners want to ensure that the balance of control over the business is not upset by one owner purchasing the interests of the other owners.

- Restrictions are necessary in order to ensure the eligibility of a corporation for, and/or status as, an "S corporation" for income tax purposes.

In addition, the owners often wish to provide mechanisms by which they might be able to obtain liquidity for their interests, and will often supplement transfer restrictions with "buy–sell" provisions, which provide for the sale of an interest by an owner to the entity and/or the other owners upon the occurrence of certain events—for example, the death or termination of employment of the owner—on terms and conditions agreed to in advance. Like transfer restrictions, buy–sell provisions serve a number of purposes for the closely held business and its owners, such as:

- Regulating ownership and control of the business and, in some cases, ensuring that ownership is confined to persons active in the business
- Preserving the balance of ownership and control among the owners
- Preventing disputes if an owner wishes, or is compelled by circumstances beyond his or her control, to terminate his or her relationship with the business
- Establishing a mechanism for dealing with disputes which might arise among the owners and for protecting the interests of minority owners
- Establishing a mechanism for valuing the business and establishing a price at which ownership interests may be transferred within the ownership group and
- Establishing a fixed value of the ownership interests for estate tax purposes and ensuring liquidity for the interest of a deceased owner.

Negotiation Considerations

The most costeffective, although not necessarily the easiest, way to negotiate a buy–sell agreement is for all of the owners to meet with an experienced attorney, keeping in mind the necessity for the attorney to avoid conflicts of interest, and attempt to reach agreement on the basic points to be covered in the agreement. The key issues that must be discussed among the parties include:

- Restrictions on lifetime transfers
- Procedures for dealing with involuntary lifetime transfers, such as transfers by operation of law upon divorce of one of the owners
- Buy–sell arrangements on death of owners
- Buy–sell arrangements on the occurrence of other events, such as termination of employment or deadlock
- Determination of the purchase price and selection of valuation procedures
- Manner of payment
- Funding strategies, including the use of life insurance proceeds to pay for the interest of a deceased owner; and
- Whether or not the agreement should cover other issues relating to management of the business, including selection of directors and officers, and the required consensus for approval of certain actions and other topics usually covered in a shareholder's agreement.

Each of these "issues" has their own subset of decisions. For example, as to each buy–sell arrangement, consideration should be given to whether there will be "optional" or "mandatory" purchases and sales and, in the case of options, which parties (i.e., the prospective seller or purchaser(s)) will have the option.

Ethical and Professional Considerations

When the founders ask the attorney who has been assisting them in forming and organizing their new corporation to take on drafting a buy–sell agreement he or she is placed in the uncomfortable position of providing legal advice to all of them, a situation that is immediately problematic given that there are a number of areas where the interests of the owners may differ. The possibility of a conflict among the owners is particularly high when there are differences in age, personal wealth, and expectations regarding the type and duration of activities of the owners with respect to the corporation and its business. Before counsel attempts to prepare a buy–sell agreement for multiple shareholders and the corporation, reference should be made to the relevant state rules of professional conduct and ethics. In addition to the concerns about conflicts of interest, counsel must be sure that he or she is competent to advise the owners regarding certain substantive legal issues relating to the decisions made about the procedures in a buy–sell agreement. One area that immediately comes to mind is tax, both income and estate, since the tax consequences to the founders may vary significantly depending on how the purchase and sale of an ownership interest in the corporation is structured. Counsel should always obtain a written acknowledgment from all of the owners regarding potential conflicts and their consent to such representation and the attorney should also be sure that the founders all realize that they can and should seek the advice of their own counsel with respect to the terms of the buy–sell agreement.

Voluntary Lifetime Transfers

In most cases, the fundamental purpose of a buy–sell agreement will be to control voluntary transfers of ownership interests in the corporation, including sales of interests and gifts. While it is possible to attempt to impose outright restrictions on such transfers, it is more common to include provisions such as:

- Conditioning transfers on the consent of the corporation, the other shareholders, or another person, and/or compliance with various procedural requirements
- Prohibiting transfers to designated persons or classes of persons, such as competitors
- Restricting transfers other than to designated persons, a group usually referred to in the agreement as "qualified purchasers"
- A "right of first offer," which obligates the shareholder to offer the corporation or the other shareholders an opportunity to acquire the restricted interest before the shareholder attempts to find an outside buyer

- A "right of first refusal," which gives the corporation or the other shareholders the right to purchase the restricted interest on the same terms as contained in any bona fide offer that the shareholder has obtained from a third party
- An obligation on the corporation or other persons to either purchase the restricted interest on terms established in the agreement or liquidate the business; or
- Providing the other shareholders with the opportunity to participate in the sale through the use of "tag-along" or "co-sale" rights.

Of course, combinations of various provisions can, and often are, used, such as creating a class of "qualified purchasers" and also requiring that transfers to anyone not meeting the definition of a "qualified purchaser" must be approved by the other shareholders.

Forms of Buy–Sell Arrangements

While transfer restrictions are directed at regulating transfers of shares outside of the initial shareholder group, buy–sell arrangements contemplate either repurchase of interests by the corporation or transfer of interests within the initial shareholder group upon the occurrence of certain events. As with restrictions on transfers, there are a number of different general forms of buy-sell arrangements, such as the following:

An "option to purchase," under which the corporation and/or the other shareholders are given the option to buy an shareholder's interest upon the occurrence of specified events as to the shareholder

- A mandatory obligation, referred to as a "buy-out," under which the interest of the shareholder must be sold to, and purchased by, the corporation and/or the other shareholders upon specified events as to the shareholder
- A "put" right, under which a shareholder may demand that the corporation and/or the other shareholders purchase the shareholder's interest upon the occurrence of specified events
- A "call" right, under which the corporation and/or the other shareholders may demand that a shareholder sell his or her interest upon the occurrence of specified events.

Two or more buy–sell arrangements may be used in one agreement, and the parties may use different arrangements depending on the particular event. The parties may also include various methods for inducing parties to take certain actions, such as providing for dissolution if an option to purchase is not exercised.

Selecting the Purchaser

A key decision in structuring any buy–sell arrangement is selecting the parties who will have either the option or the obligation to purchase a shareholder's ownership interest upon the occurrence of certain events. The first option is the so-called *redemption agreement*, which provides the corporation with either the option or the obligation to purchase the interest of a shareholder upon the occurrence of certain specified events. In most situations, the redemption agreement will apply to proposed lifetime transfers and will require that a shareholder who wishes to sell his or her interest to a person who is not already a shareholder must first offer the interest to the corporation either at a price and terms that are fixed in advance in the agreement or at a price and terms similar to that already offered by the outside buyer. The redemption agreement usually also comes into play on the death of the shareholder, at which time the estate of decedent will be required to offer his interest for sale to the corporation on terms and at a price set in the agreement.

The second option is a "crosspurchase agreement," which provides each shareholder with either the option or the obligation to purchase the interest of the other shareholders upon the occurrence of certain specified events. For example, if a shareholder wishes to sell his or her interest to a person who is not already a shareholder, he or she must first offer to sell it to the other shareholders in the same manner described above for a redemption agreement. A cross-purchase agreement usually also comes into play on the death of an shareholder, at which time the estate of decedent will be required to offer the decedent's interest for sale to the surviving shareholders on terms and at a price set in the agreement. Whenever the shareholders have an option or obligation to purchase the interest of another shareholder under a cross-purchase agreement, the rights and burdens will generally be distributed pro rata among them in proportion to their share ownership; however, it is also possible to establish various priorities within the shareholder group.

The third option is a "hybrid agreement," which combines the elements of redemption and cross-purchase agreements. In a hybrid agreement, each shareholder agrees to offer his interest for sale to the corporation and to the other shareholders upon the occurrence of certain specified events, and to have his or her estate offer it for sale to both the corporation and the other shareholders at death. There are a number of ways in which the rights and burdens can be allocated between the corporation and the other shareholders, such as successive options to the corporation and then the other shareholders, or vice versa, or options in the other shareholders coupled with the corporation's obligation to purchase any remaining interest.

A number of tax and nontax factors should be considered in selecting the purchaser or purchasers in any buy–sell agreement, including the sources available for funding the purchase of the interest; the number of shareholders of the business; and the ages and proportionate ownership interests of the shareholders.

Buy–Sell Events

The parties must carefully consider which events may come within the scope of the buy–sell agreement and trigger a right or obligation to sell or purchase the shares of the shareholder to which the event pertains. Buy–sell agreements can cover a wide range of events that may occur in the personal and professional lives of the shareholders. The most common "trigger events" are proposed lifetime sales to outsiders and the death of a shareholder; however, buy–sell provisions may be made applicable in a number of other situations such gifts, transfers to family members or other shareholders, involuntary lifetime transfers, termination of employment for various reasons (e.g., voluntary retirement, discharge and/or disability), change-in-control transactions, deadlocks, and a desire to terminate the business relationship with other shareholders.

Transfers at death, along with restrictions on voluntary lifetime transfers, receive the most attention in any buy–sell agreement. The most common provision for transfers at death is the mandatory offer, under which the estate of the deceased shareholder must offer to sell the decedent's interest to the corporation, the other shareholders or both, depending on the type of agreement that has been selected. This type of mandatory offer is required to fix estate tax valuation. However, it is not necessary for the other parties to be obligated to buy the offered interest, although it is customary to provide for the mandatory buy-out of the interest funded through life insurance. If the agreement is not being used to fix estate tax values, it may restrict the class of permissible transferees at death, generally to other parties to the agreement or to specified family members of the deceased. The agreement should include provisions designed to ensure that the decedent's executor and legal representative adhere to the terms of the agreement, and that any heirs, successors, or assignees will remain bound by the agreement.

When the success of a closely held business depends on the continued active involvement of the shareholders as employees, it is not surprising that many buy–sell agreements include options in favor of the corporation and/or the other shareholders to purchase the interest of a shareholder who ceases to be employed in the business. While many agreements simply refer generally to terminations, without regard to the particular circumstances, it often makes sense to explicitly distinguish among the events listed on the slide and establish different buy–sell arrangements for each form of termination. For example, repurchase at "fair value" in an "all cash" deal payable at closing may be required when an shareholder is terminated without "cause" or retires at or after a specified retirement age while shareholders who are terminated "for cause" or retire early may have no right to have their interests purchased or may only be offered an amount equal to their cost for the interest that would be payable in installments over several years under the terms of a promissory note.

The ability to purchase the interest of a departed shareholder-employee can be quite advantageous for the business and the other shareholders. For example, the repurchased interest can be used to recruit a replacement for the departing shareholder. Also, the other shareholders can be freed from the burdens of continuing to comply with the rights otherwise given to minority shareholders, such as inspection and voting rights. The departed shareholder-employee may also be eager to sell a minority interest, since it is unlikely that he or she will ever be able to again exercise any meaningful influence over the ongoing operation of the business.

CHAPTER 6

Founders and Organizational Culture

Introduction

Not surprisingly, there are differences of opinion regarding the definition of organizational culture and how it develops. Schein offers one useful definition of the term by declaring that

> [o]rganizational culture . . . is the pattern of basic assumptions that a given group has invented, discovered, or developed in learning to cope with its problems of external adaptation and internal integration—a pattern of assumptions that has worked well enough to be considered valid and, therefore, to be taught to new members as the correct way to perceive, think, and feel in relation to those problems.[1]

Schein has noted that the founders of an organization not only create the group but also launch the process of defining and shaping the group's "organizational culture" through the force of their own personalities and by applying their own theories about how the organization can be successful based on their own previous experiences in the cultures in which

---

[1] Schein, E. 1983. "The Role of the Founder in Creating Organizational Culture." In *Organizational Dynamics* 348–64, 348. New York, NY: American Management Association. For further discussion of organizational culture, see "Organizational Culture: A Library of Resources for Sustainable Entrepreneurs" prepared and distributed by the Sustainable Entrepreneurship Project (www.seproject.org).

they grew up.[2] Schein cautions that while founders may prepare and disseminate formal "charters" that describe their preferred philosophy or value system, the actual organizational culture is the assumptions that underlie the values and which have been embraced by the organizational members in a way that determines acceptable behaviors by those members. In other words, while the assumptions and theories that the founders bring to the group are important they will be tested by the actual experiences of the group before they are ultimately accepted as part of the organizational culture.[3]

Role of Founders in Creating Organizational Culture

The role of the founders with respect to creating the organizational culture can be understood by following the "typical" progression of the firm as suggested by Schein. The first step, of course, is the identification of an idea for a new enterprise by a single person—the "founder." While the founder could presumably act on his or her idea without the help of others, what generally happens is that others are brought into what becomes a "founding group" that operates based on a consensus that the idea is viable and worth pursuing even in the face of known and unknown risks and uncertainties. The founding group begins to take the necessary steps to launch and organize the firm, including obtaining capital, forming a business entity (e.g., a corporation), preparing and filing patent applications, and other things. As the launch process unfolds and resources become available the founding group brings other necessary parties into the process, including employees and external advisors and business partners, and the group begins to cope with its problems of external adaptation and internal integration and gather the information necessary to settle upon an organizational culture.[4]

---

[2] Schein, E. 1983. "The Role of the Founder in Creating Organizational Culture." In *Organizational Dynamics* 348–64, 348–49. New York, NY: American Management Association.

[3] Id. ("The ultimate organizational culture will always reflect the complex interaction between (1) the assumptions and theories that founders bring to the group initially and (2) what the group learns subsequently from its own experiences.").

[4] Id. at p. 352.

While the actual experiences of the group in coping with external adaptation and internal integration will determine which values and assumptions are accepted as part of the group's organizational culture, Schein had no doubt that the founder will have a strong influence for several reasons. First of all, the initial idea for the enterprise will almost certainly be accompanied by strong views about how the idea can be fulfilled and those views will be a by-product of the founder's personality and his or her previous experiences in other cultural contexts. Second, the founders observed by Schein were generally quite strong-minded about what should be done and how it should be done and this included "strong assumptions about the nature of the world, the role their organization will play in the world, the human nature, truth, relationships, time, and space." In other words, founders bring to their role of organizational leader a distinct and pre-determined "view of the world." Finally, the founder, in his or her role as the president or other titular leader of the group during the formation process, will necessarily have a strong influence on the strategies that are used to address the firm's initial set of external survival and internal integration problems.[5]

Founder's Methods for Embedding Preferred Cultural Elements

Schein noted that in order for the founder to be successful in injecting his or her preferred values and assumptions into the organizational culture he or she must first determine the best way to "teach" those values and assumptions to other members of the group. Once the teaching process has been perfected group members can express their views as to whether or not those values and assumptions will work in overcoming the problems—external and internal—threatening the survival of the group. Schein suggested the following list of "mechanisms" that founders and other key organizational leaders can use to "embed" their preferred cultural elements within the group[6]:

---

[5] Id.

[6] Id. at p. 355 (Figure 3).

1. Formal statements of organizational philosophy, charters, creeds, materials used for recruitment and selection, and socialization.
2. Design of physical spaces, facades, and buildings.
3. Deliberate role modeling, teaching, and coaching by leaders.
4. Explicit reward and status system and promotion criteria.
5. Stories, legends, myths, and parables about key people and events.
6. What leaders pay attention to, measure, and control.
7. Leader reactions to critical incidents and organizational crises (times when organizational survival is threatened, norms are unclear or are challenged, insubordination occurs, threatening or meaningless events occur, and so forth).
8. How the organization is designed and structured. (The design of work, who reports to whom, degree of decentralization, functional or other criteria for differentiation, and mechanisms used for integration carry implicit messages of what leaders assume and value.)
9. Organizational systems and procedures. (The types of information, control, and decision support systems in terms of categories of information, time cycles, who gets what information, and when and how performance appraisal and other review processes are conducted carry implicit messages of what leaders assume and value.)
10. Criteria used for recruitment, selection, promotion, leveling off, retirement, and "excommunication" of people (the implicit and possibly unconscious criteria that leaders use to determine who "fits" and who doesn't "fit" membership roles and key slots in the organization).

Schein listed the mechanisms from more or less explicit ones to more or less implicit ones and noted that the mechanisms will vary in terms of potency and effectiveness. Further complications arise from the fact that the mechanisms often are in conflict with one another, as well as the fact that different subgroups within the organization may have different assumptions about the way that the world should be viewed. Finally, as noted above, the process of "embedding" calls for teaching skills and tools and founders do not always do the best job of clearly conveying their meaning and may often unwittingly communicate implicit messages that they are not even aware of.[7]

---

[7] Id. at pp. 356–57.

Stanford Project Study of Influence of Founders on Organizational Culture

An interesting study of organizational culture among early-stage technology companies in the Silicon Valley was undertaken by the Stanford Project on Emerging Companies (SPEC).[8] Among other things the researchers were interested in how the founders of those companies addressed key organizational design issues during the startup period. The SPEC was concerned not only with the actions taken, and decisions made, as these companies were launched and began to grow but also wanted to learn more about the long-term impact of those actions and decisions on the company as it continued forward and became larger and more mature. The researchers postulated that in order for a company to be successful it was necessary to develop and institutionalize coherent blueprints for the relationship between the company and its employees that fostered reliability and accountability. They believed that the choices made by companies with respect to definition and adoption of their relational blueprint, which is an important element of their organizational culture, would be heavily influenced by the beliefs of the founders of those companies (and any nonfounder CEO) regarding how workflow within the company and the employment relationship should be structured.

Dimensions for the Creation of Organizational Blueprint

Based on extensive interviews of the founders and, where applicable, non-founder CEOs of the companies in their study group the researchers identified what they considered to be three crucial dimensions that could be used to describe and categorize how companies created a blueprint during the startup period for creating and maintaining a relationship with their employees that fostered reliability and accountability: the basis of attachment to and retention by the company; the organizational structure, as

---

[8] The discussion below is based on "Entrepreneurship: Lessons from the Stanford Project on Emerging Companies," Stanford Graduate School of Business (September 3, 2003) (hereinafter "SPEC (2003)"). Further information on the SPEC is available on the SPEC website (http://www-gsb.standord.edu/SPEC).

determined by the means selected to attempt to coordinate and control employee activities; and the criterion used for selecting persons to join the workforce. Information from the founders and nonfounder CEOs was considered crucial because the choices made by companies with respect to definition and adoption of their relational blueprint is heavily influenced by the beliefs of these key leaders regarding how work flow within the company and the employment relationship should be structured.[9]

The first dimension, "attachment," refers to the basis for the bond, or relationship, formed between a company and its employees. The SPEC researchers described three different bases for attachment—love, work, and money. Founders and CEOs wishing to rely on "love" did so by attempting to create and maintain a feeling of community and "family" within the workplace and thus forge strong emotional bonds within the workforce that would motivate employees and make them want to remain with the company. On the other hand, when attachment was based on "work" the focus was on appealing to the desire of knowledge workers to be part of an organization that provided opportunities for interesting and challenging work on cutting-edge technologies and for personal and professional development. In this type of environment, the primary loyalty of employees was to a specific project as opposed to the company, a supervisor, or other coworkers. Finally, companies where the attachment was based on "money" tended to be those where both sides looked at the employment relationship simply as an exchange of labor for money without the additional emotional connection and/or intellectual challenge associated with the other forms of attachment.[10]

The second dimension—organizational structure—is largely determined by the initial choices made by the founders and CEOs regarding the principal means used to coordinate and control the flow of work within the company. SPEC researchers found that the most commonly used method relied heavily on informal controls through peer pressure and, eventually, organizational culture; however, at least three other approaches were also identified. First, some companies relied on "professional control," which was grounded in the assumption that employees

---

[9] Id. at pp. 3–4.
[10] Id. at p. 4.

were professionally socialized to diligently perform outstanding work based on their formal education and training. Employees in these companies, which tended to have a recruiting preference for high-potential individuals from elite institutions, were given significant autonomy and independence. Second, some companies chose to implement formal procedures and systems to control employees. Finally, some founders and CEOs preferred to directly oversee the activities of their employees to control and coordinate the workflow within the company.[11]

The third and final dimension is the method used by founders and CEOs to select employees and the underlying assumption is that these company leaders will have a relatively high involvement in recruitment and selection of managers and employees at least while the size of the company remains small and they are likely to have regular direct contact with most of the employees. Once again, several distinct alternatives were identified in the course of the research. Not surprisingly, one of the popular approaches was to staff the company based on the evidence of skills and experience required in order to complete one or more of the tasks or activities that might be of immediate importance to the success of the company. This alternative is noteworthy because of its emphasis on the immediate, or short-term, needs of the company. Because startups often have less time and money than they really want or need it is essential that limited resources be invested in employees who can contribute right away and get up to speed quickly and easily without slowing down the process of developing new products or technologies. Companies that looked to grow and develop through completion of a series of projects tended to be more interested in indications of long-term potential of new employees and their apparent aptitude for easily transitioning to new and increasingly challenging projects over time. Finally, some companies, which are obviously interested in the skills and experience of prospective employees, tended to place the greatest weight on how well the candidate would apparently fit into the culture of the company and relate to coworkers.[12]

---

[11] Id. at pp. 4–5.
[12] Id. at p. 5.

Models of Employment Relations

After the SPEC had researchers identified the three types of attachment and selection and the four types of control present within the companies in the study group they moved on to study the relationships among the three dimensions in order to construct various alternative models for employment relations, a strong proxy for organizational culture, which could then be evaluated and tested on other measures. Based on how the choices made by the various companies were clustered the researchers came up with five basic models of employment relations referred to as engineering, star, commitment, bureaucracy, and autocracy.[13]

The dominant types on the three key dimensions for the "engineering" model were challenging work, peer group control, and selection based on the ability to perform specific tasks. The engineering model conforms closely to the standard descriptions of the basic Silicon Valley model and was, in fact, the most common model among the SPEC study group. Companies formed on the "engineering" evidenced a strong commitment to the project-at-hand, if not the company itself as was the case with the "commitment" model. Employees were attracted to these types of companies by the need to work on closely knit teams dedicated to resolution of difficult and challenging problems. Employees were performance-driven and achievement-oriented and able and willing to work on interdisciplinary teams that were formed for a particular project and then disbanded when work on the project was completed. These companies tended to have a high level of customer focus when selecting their projects. Accordingly, as customer preferences changed the selection criterion for employees had to be modified also in order to ensure that the available personnel were qualified for the current tasks.[14]

The dominant types on the three key dimensions for the "star" model were challenging work, professional control, and selection based on long-term potential. The star model aligns closely with the way in which research work is conducted in academia and it is not surprising that this model was by far the most popular with those companies that were

---

[13] Id. at pp. 5–6.
[14] Id. at p. 6.

engaged in medical technology and research, including biotechnology. Only a very small percentage of the companies that were active in other industrial sectors chose the star model. Recruiting policies and strategies at companies following the "star" model focused on identifying candidates with the highest level of talent and accomplishment, paying them top wages and providing them with the autonomy and resources that they needed in order to accomplish their immediate goals and continue to develop as experts in their fields. For founders the challenge was to establish and maintain an exciting environment and find a way to balance their need for control against the autonomy demanded by talented employees attracted to that particular employment model.[15]

The dominant types on the three key dimensions for the "commitment" model were emotional and familial links between the company and its employees (i.e., "love"), peer group control, and selection based on cultural fit. Anecdotally, the most well-known and celebrated example of the commitment model within Silicon Valley has been the early years of Hewlett Packard. It was common for the founders of companies based on the "commitment" model to speak of their personal involvement in the simplest aspects of the company and its relations with employees including personal visits with employees on a regular basis and down-to-earth involvement in company events. For these founders the goal was to encourage lifetime employment and commitment to the company, its missions, and the people who worked there.[16]

The dominant types on the three key dimensions for the "bureaucracy" model were challenging work, formalized control, and selection based on the ability to perform specific tasks. Not surprisingly, these "bureaucratic" companies based their operations on specific procedures, methodologies and systems, and the founders and human resources managers invested a significant amount of time and effort in creating documentation including job and product descriptions. Formal and rigorous project management systems and tools were also a hallmark of companies using the "bureaucracy" model.[17]

---

[15] Id. at pp. 6–7.

[16] Id.

[17] Id. at p. 6.

The dominant types on the three key dimensions for the "autocracy" model were exchange of labor for money, control through personal oversight, and selection based on the ability to perform specific tasks. Not surprisingly, founders depending on the "autocracy" model tended to have little skill with, or patience for, slow and deliberative consensus management techniques. While founders believed that employees communicated well, there was little time for the warm and fuzzy interactions associated with the commitment model and there was little delegation of authority or doubt in the minds of employees as to who would be making the final decisions on key issues.[18] Like the "bureaucracy" model, autocratic founders did not invest a lot of time in interactions with employees, relied on formalized controls to guide day-to-day activities, and tended not to delegate substantial amounts of authority with respect to key decisions relating to the company.[19]

Several observations can be made regarding the five basic models. First, the "commitment" model is unique because it is the only that relies heavily on "love" and forging a sense of community among the employees as the basis for creating and maintaining a relationship between the employees and the company. Second, the "autocracy" model is unique for other reasons given that it is alone in its preferences with regard to attachment ("money") and coordination and control (i.e., direct monitoring). Third, quality of work and skills were the most popular choices for attachment and selection, respectively. Finally, the "engineering" and "bureaucracy" models were the closest of the five basic models differing only with respect to their approach to coordination and control (i.e., peer and/or cultural control for engineering-type companies and formal processes and procedures for bureaucracy-type companies).[20]

Obviously not all of the companies in the SPEC study conformed exactly to one of the basic models. The SPEC researchers identified a number of "near-model" types, which were cases where companies differed from one (and only one) of the basic models on only one dimension. For example, a founder might attempt to base attachment on love,

---

[18] Id. at p. 11.
[19] Id. at pp. 13–15.
[20] Id. at p. 42.

exercise control through personal oversight, and select employees based on cultural fit. This combination was very close to the "commitment" model, with the only difference being the basis upon which control was exercised over employees. Also, while the researchers were confident about the value of identifying the various basic models they also acknowledged that some companies followed what was referred to as a "nontype" blueprint because they differed from two or more basic model types on one dimension or differed along two or more dimensions from every basic model type.[21]

Factors Influencing Selection of Employment Relations Model

Of the models discussed above, the most common among the study group was the engineering model; however, one of the most striking features of the results of the SPEC study is the remarkable diversity among the companies in spite of their common roots within the mythical Silicon Valley culture and the related business and social network. A number of theories on organizational development argue against the high level of diversity found among the companies in the SPEC study group. For example, neo-institutionalists that have studied the development and growth of Silicon Valley have predicted that companies will adopt specific corporate structures and practices because of the profound influence of venture capitalists, human resource professionals, and the law and accounting firms that advise those companies.[22] While the SPEC researchers concede that companies receiving venture capital are more likely to bureaucratize more often and at an earlier stage,[23] in general the companies that have been

---

[21] Id. at pp. 6–7.

[22] Id. at p. 9 (citing Suchman, M.C. 2000. "Dealmakers and Counselors: Law Firms as Intermediaries in the Development of Silicon Valley." In *Understanding Silicon Valley: The Anatomy of an Entrepreneurial Region*, ed. M. Kenney, 70–97. Stanford, CA: Stanford University Press).

[23] Id. at p. 9 (citing Baron, J.N., M. Burton, and M. Hannan. 1999. "Engineering Bureaucracy: The Genesis of Formal Policies, Positions, and Structures in High-Technology Firms." *Journal of Law, Economics and Organization* 15, no. 1, pp. 1–41).

supported by venture capitalists in the study group evidenced substantial diversity in the organizational blueprints. This does not necessarily mean that venture capitalists did not have any influence upon the strategies and structures selected by their portfolio companies. In fact, many venture capitalists, in an attempt to differentiate themselves in what is often a very competitive marketplace where investors fight to get into promising new deals, are well known for their preferences for certain corporate cultures. One can identify venture capitalists that prefer to be associated with companies that are being built to survive based on long-term emotional ties, similar to the "commitment" model, while others are more interested in "star" cultures or companies that value technological excellence and structure their organizations and selection processes accordingly.[24]

Interestingly the SPEC researchers did not find any consistent correlation between the employment models selected by the founders and the founder's own professional background working within other organizations. For example, while there were founders within the sample group who came from bureaucratic organizations and chose to adopt a bureaucratic template there were also a similar number of founders coming from the same background who specifically rejected bureaucracy as dysfunctional and expressed a keen desire to embrace a completely different culture and operating style for their new companies.[25] On the other hand, however, there did appear to be a link between the organizational blueprint selected and the founder's initial business strategy. The companies in the SPEC study group generally chose one of five specific business strategies—radical innovation (49 percent); technology enhancement (20 percent); sales, marketing, or service (14 percent); cost minimization (7 percent); or a hybrid (10 percent). Companies that selected radical innovation tended to select either the "star" or "engineering" models. Companies that selected technology enhancement tended to select the "star," "engineering," or "bureaucracy" models. Companies that selected sales, marketing, or service preferred the "commitment," "engineering," or "bureaucracy" models. Finally, companies that selected cost minimization preferred either the "engineering" or "autocracy" models.

---

[24] Id. at pp. 9–10.
[25] Id. at p. 10.

While one could find engineering companies that tried to compete through each of the four main business strategies, companies following the commitment model tended to limit their business strategy to sales, marketing, or service, a path that was consistent with the emphasis of those types of companies on establishing close long-term relationships between the company and its employees, which, in turn, could support the strategic objective of strong long-term relationships between those committed employees and the company's key customers. Similarly, "autocratic" companies limited their business strategy to cost minimization.[26] This data is consistent with the view of many commentators that strategy is an important factor in organizational design generally and specifically in selecting the appropriate form of organizational culture.

Impact of Initial Employment Relations Model on Firm Evolution

The SPEC researchers claimed that the results of their study provided evidence that the choices made by the founders with respect to the initial employment blueprint did have a strong impact on the evolution of the company and that attempts to significantly alter the blueprint as the company mature would likely have a substantial destabilizing effect. A little over half of the companies in the SPEC study group made no changes in their organizational blueprint as they evolved while another 30 percent changed on just one dimension, usually to control coordination. About 15 percent of the companies attempted to change from one of the pure model types to another, although almost three-quarters of these changes were between the closely related "engineering" and "bureaucracy" models.[27] The researchers tested differences between the preferences of the founders and the nonfounder CEOs who were more likely to come on board a significant amount of time after the founders have launched the company and the original employment blueprint was selected and applied. The key findings appear to be that the star and engineering models were more popular with founders than with the CEO group and that

---

[26] Id. at pp. 11–12.
[27] Id. at pp. 12–13.

the CEO group was more likely than the founder group to prefer the bureaucracy model.[28] However, in general, the founder's views regarding the appropriate level of self-management were generally so well engrained during the startup phase that later attempts by a new CEO to introduce more formal bureaucratic procedures were typically not very successful and were often dangerously destabilizing to the business.[29]

Companies that adopted the commitment model took on lower levels of administrative overhead as they developed and matured[30]; were more likely to go public, relative to comparable companies that selected different models; and were also the least likely to "fail," which included declaring bankruptcy, being acquiring on unfavorable terms, or simply shutting the doors and disappearing without a formal closure.[31] Companies that selected the star model were least likely to go public; however, star model companies that did go public enjoyed the highest levels of stock market performance once the IPO was completed. Star model companies fared second best, behind the commitment model companies, in their ability to avoid failure.[32] Companies that selected the autocratic model were most likely to fail and if they were able to survive and complete an IPO they turned in the worst post-IPO stock market performance. The second worst performance came from those companies that had no clear model. It should be noted, however, that apart from the striking strengths of the commitment model with respect to completing an IPO and avoiding failure, the differences among the other models were not that significant.[33]

---

[28] Id. at p. 44.

[29] Id. at p. 13.

[30] Id at p. 13 (citing Baron, J., M. Burton, and M. Hannan. 1999. "Engineering Bureaucracy: The Genesis of Formal Policies, Positions, and Structures in High-Technology Firms." *Journal of Law, Economics, and Organization* 15, no. 1, pp. 1–41).

[31] Id. at pp. 14–15 (citing Hannan, M., J. Baron, G. Hsu, and O. Kocak. 2006. *Staying the Course: Early Organization Building and the Success of High-Technology Firms. Unpublished Manuscript.* Graduate School of Business, Stanford University).

[32] Id.

[33] Id. at p. 15.

In general, the two most unattractive models for Silicon Valley-based companies were the "bureaucratic" and "autocratic" blueprints.

As noted above, material changes in the initial organizational blueprint were relatively uncommon among the companies in the SPEC study group; however, the researchers nonetheless attempt to assess and understand the relationship between attempts to change the organizational culture and "destabilization," which can take a variety of different forms including erosion of skills and talents due to turnover, sudden and extreme alterations in the bases of power and status within the company; undermining of cherished belief systems; confusion in the minds of outsiders, such as customers, investors, and other business partners, about the identity and purposes of the company; and damage to the reputation of the company.[34] They found that companies that significantly changed their employment blueprint after the start-up stage were much more likely to fail and if those companies had completed an IPO before the change they could expect to experience a substantial decrease in their market value following the change.[35] There was a strong positive correlation between changes in the initial employment blueprint and employee turnover, particularly turnover among the more senior employees.[36] Not surprisingly, the higher the level of turnover the more adverse impact there was on subsequent growth in the revenues of the company. When changes were made to the initial employment blueprint a change to the engineering model was generally the least disruptive. In general, however, changing the model typically reduced the likelihood of a successful IPO by 50 percent, tripled the likelihood of failure, and triggered rapid deterioration in subsequent growth of the market capitalization of the company.

---

[34] Id. at p. 13.

[35] Id. at p. 16 (citing Hannan, M., J.N. Baron, G. Hsu, and O. Kocak. 2006. "Staying the Course: Early Organization Building and the Success of High-Technology Firms." *Unpublished Manuscript*. Graduate School of Business, Stanford University).

[36] Id. at p. 13 (citing Baron, J.N., M.T. Hannan, and M.D. Burton. 2001. "Labor Pains: Organizational Change and Employee Turnover in Young, High-Tech Firms." *American Journal of Sociology* 106, no. 4, pp. 960–1012).

Founder's Influence on Organizational Design

Organizational development has been widely and intensely studied and researchers have been particularly interested in how external and internal contingencies confronting organizations as they grow and mature influence organizational design, particularly the level of bureaucratization.[37] Several researchers have observed that the amount, form, and timing of bureaucratization as organizations develop and mature is significantly impacted by the circumstances surrounding the founding of the organization, particularly the influences of the founders, and the "embedded" social relationships that took hold among the original members of the organization.[38] In addition, Weber, the most prominent student of "bureaucracy," argued that preexisting foundations of authority, which are often established and nurtured by the founders and their followers (e.g., charismatic, traditional, or rational-legal), and social and economic context are two significant factors in predicting the form and character of bureaucratic institutions.[39]

---

[37] For detailed discussion of organizational design, see "Organizational Design" in "Entrepreneurship: A Library of Resources for Sustainable Entrepreneurs" and "Organizational Design: A Library of Resources for Sustainable Entrepreneurs," both prepared and distributed by the Sustainable Entrepreneurship Project (www.seproject.org).

[38] Baron, J., M. Burton, and M. Hannan. 1999. "Engineering Bureaucracy: The Genesis of Formal Policies, Positions and Structures in High-Technology Firms." *The Journal of Law, Economics and Organization* 15, no. 2, pp. 1–41 (citing Boeker, W. 1988. "Organizational Origins: Entrepreneurial and Environmental Imprinting at the Time of Founding." In *Ecological Models of Organizations*, ed. G. Carroll, 33–51. Cambridge, MA: Ballinger; and Granovetter, M. 1985. "Economic Action and Social Structure: the Problem of Embeddedness." *American Journal of Sociology* 91, no. 3, pp. 481–510). Baron et al. commented that the results of their research provided evidence "that organizational architecture is shaped by social characteristics of, and relations among, the early 'occupants' of the structures being designed" and took specific note of the significant negative relationship between the early representation of women in their sample of high technology firms and the level of specialization of managerial and administrative roles in those firms. Id. at p. 14.

[39] Baron, J., M. Burton, and M. Hannan. 1999. "Engineering Bureaucracy: The Genesis of Formal Policies, Positions and Structures in High-Technology Firms."

Baron et al. used data collected from the companies in the SPEC study group to analyze the influence of founders on several facets of "bureaucratization," specifically managerial intensity, the formalization of employment policies and relationships and the proliferation of specialized managerial and administrative roles and titles.[40] In selecting their areas of study, the researchers noted that they focused on several attributes of bureaucratization that scholars had previously identified as "defining aspects of the bureaucratic form," including the following elements: formal definition (and increasing specialization) of fixed and official jurisdictional areas; reliance on hierarchical authority vested in formal roles; formalization and documentation of rules; selection of personnel based on qualifications; employment viewed as a career and governed by explicit and well-documented rules and procedures; and the emergence of management and administration as a "role," conducted full-time as a professional vocation, which is discharged universally and dispassionately.[41] The researchers concluded that the organizational models that arose under the influence of the founders, as well as the social composition of the labor force at the time of founding, had a significant impact on the growth in managerial intensity among the firms, an impact that endured even after the initial founders were no longer with the firm.[42] However, the

---

The Journal of Law, Economics and Organization 15, no. 2, pp. 1–41 (citing Weber, M. 1946. "Bureaucracy." In *From Max Weber: Essays in Sociology*, eds. H. Gerth and C. Mills, 196–244. New York, NY: Oxford University Press).

[40] Baron, J., M. Burton, and M. Hannan. 1999. "Engineering Bureaucracy: The Genesis of Formal Policies, Positions and Structures in High-Technology Firms." *The Journal of Law, Economics and Organization* 15, no.1, pp. 1–41.

[41] Id. at p. 3 (citing Max Weber's list of several of the quintessential elements of "bureaucracy" described in Scott, W. 1992. *Organizations: Rational, Natural and Open Systems*, 40–41. 3rd ed. Englewood Cliffs, NJ: Prentice Hall).

[42] Id. at pp. 1 and 3–4. Baron et al. noted that these findings were consistent with the observations of other researchers who had observed that the amount, form and timing of bureaucratization as organizations develop and mature is significantly impacted by the circumstances surrounding the founding of the organization, particularly the influences of the founders, and the "embedded" social relationships that took hold among the original members of the organization. See, for example, Boeker, W. 1988. "Organizational Origins: Entrepreneurial and Environmental Imprinting at the Time of Founding." In *Ecological*

researchers found less evidence of founder influence on the formalization of employment policies and relationships and the proliferation of specialized management titles. In fact, they argued that these "superficial aspects of bureaucracy" were eventually adopted as a result of normal organizational growth and maturity and to satisfy "external gatekeepers," such as venture capitalists, analysts, and institutional investors.[43]

Managerial intensity refers to the degree to which an organization depends on managerial and administrative specialists and follows Scott's definition of bureaucracy "as the existence of a specialized administrative staff."[44] Baron et al. measured the "prevalence of specialized managerial and administrative functions and personnel" by looking at the number of full-time equivalent managerial and administrative specialists employed by firms in their study group.[45] They found, as expected, that firms founded on the basis of a bureaucratic model had the highest level of managerial intensity while firms with founders that followed the commitment model (i.e., relying on implicit and informal controls and alignment of the interests of the firm and its workers through long-term attachments) exhibited much lower levels of administrative intensity.[46] As an aside, Baron et al. commented that the relatively low reliance on specialized managerial and administrative functions and personnel among "commitment" firms did not necessarily mean that the founder had abandoned efforts at coordination and control and that oversight and monitoring may have come

---

Models of Organizations, ed. G. Carroll, 33–51. Cambridge, MA: Ballinger; and Granovetter, M. 1985. "Economic Action and Social Structure: the Problem of Embeddedness." *American Journal of Sociology* 91, no. 3, pp. 481–510.

[43] Id.

[44] Scott, W. 1992. "Organizations: Rational." *Natural and Open Systems*, 40. 3rd ed. Englewood Cliffs, NJ: Prentice Hall.

[45] Baron, J., M. Burton, and M. Hannan. 1999. "Engineering Bureaucracy: The Genesis of Formal Policies, Positions and Structures in High-Technology Firms." *The Journal of Law, Economics and Organization* 15, no.1, pp. 1–41, 3 and 9.

[46] Id. at pp. 3 and 10. See also Walton, R. 1985. "From Control to Commitment in the Workplace." *Harvard Business Review* 63, no. 2, pp. 76–84 (arguing that organizations structured along clan or commitment lines can reduce the amount of bureaucratic overhead).

in any form such as reliance on budgets, information systems, or other similar types of controls.[47]

Evidence was also found that the proportional representation of women among the firm workforce at the end of the first year of operations had a statistically significant negative effect on managerial-administrative intensity.[48] The researchers found that the average percentage of women included in the senior management team was 14 percent and that senior women were typically toiling in human resources and administration and much less likely to be found overseeing engineering or research and development activities.[49] When the spotlight was placed on the top of the organizational hierarchy the researchers found that only about 10 percent of the studied companies had a woman occupying the role of CEO, president, or founder. Gender diversity at the top of the organizational hierarchy did have an impact on hiring policies for other roles within the company as the researchers found that when there was a woman at the top of the pyramid the company, or leading the engineering or research and development functions, it was much more likely that the company would have more women in scientific and technical positions.

Formalization of employment policies and relationships was measured analyzing the level and timing of adoption of various employment practices, policies, forms, and documents directed at formalization of some aspect of the employment relationship. Specifically, the person most knowledgeable about human resources matters at each firm was surveyed about which of the following items had been adopted by the end of the first year of firm operations and by the time the researchers made their first visit to the firm: organization chart; standardized employment application; written job descriptions; personnel manual or handbook; written employment tests; written performance evaluations; standard performance evaluation forms; written affirmative action plans; standard employment contract for exempt employees; employee grievance or complaint forms;

---

[47] Id. at p. 10 (footnote 9).

[48] Id. at pp. 3 and 13.

[49] Baron, J., M. Hannan, G. Hsu, and O. Kocak. 2007. "In The Company of Women: Gender Inequality and the Logic of Bureaucracy in Start-Up Firms." *Work and Occupations* 34, no.1, pp. 35–66.

and human resources information system. While the researchers found that firms had, on average, adopted few, if any, of the aforementioned items by the end of their first year, by the time that the survey team visited firms had, on average, adopted between six and seven of the practices.[50] Baron et al. concluded that "[o]n balance . . . we find less evidence of enduring effects of founder's models on the extent or pace of employment formalization than we did on the evolution of managerial-administrative intensity."[51] They noted that in the this area it was not a question of whether technology firms would adopt formal human resources practices but how fast would they do it and pointed out that receipt of venture capital investment tended to accelerate the adoption process.

Formalization and specialization of top management roles was measured by looking at the extent to which the following positions had been created in the firm's organizational hierarchy by the end of the first year of firm operations and by the time the researchers made their first visit to the firm: President; Chief Executive Officer; Chief Operating Officer; Chief Financial Officer' Chief Technical Officer; Chief Information Officer; Vice President, Engineering (R&D, Technology); Vice President, Sales; Vice President, Marketing; Vice President, Customer Support/Service; Vice President, Operations (Manufacturing, Production); Vice President, Finance; Vice President, Administration; Vice President, Human Resources; Vice President, Strategic Planning (Business Development); and/or "Senior" or "Executive" titles in any of the vice presidential areas.[52] The researchers found a relatively weak relationship between founding conditions and formalization and specialization of top management roles and commented that increases in the proliferation of management titles

---

[50] Baron, J., M. Burton, and M. Hannan. 1999. "Engineering Bureaucracy: The Genesis of Formal Policies, Positions and Structures in High-Technology Firms." *The Journal of Law, Economics and Organization* 15, no. 1, pp. 1–41. Interestingly, 64 percent of the firms had not adopted any of the employment practices during their first year and only 23 percent adopted more than one of the practices during their first year. Id.

[51] Id. at p. 23.

[52] Id. at p. 24 (also describing how the researchers handled categorization issues such as different titles and persons holding multiple titles).

was more strongly driven by factors such as employment growth, venture capital funding, and going public.[53]

Founder's Networks

It has long been contended that in order for organizations to form and prosper the organization must have access to sufficient resources of wealth, power, and legitimacy.[54] Since a new organization does not have its own network, this means that during its initial organizational stages it is heavily, if not exclusively, dependent on the then-existing social networks of the organizational founders and the efforts of those founders to tap into those networks and expand them in ways that can help support the launch of the organization.[55] Powell and Porter described these social networks as consisting of "relational ties that foster the flow of a wide variety of resources among individuals" and which "enable individuals to engage in activities that would be much more difficult (if not impossible) if they were not socially connected to the person with whom they were interacting."[56]

The importance of social networks and the resources they can provide to new organizations has been validated by various studies.[57] For example,

---

[53] Id. at p. 28. The researchers noted that this was consistent with arguments of other researchers that development of bureaucratic organizational characteristics accelerates with the introduction of outside stakeholders, such as venture capitalists and institutional investors, in order for the firm to appear credible in the eyes of those stakeholders. The survey included evidence that firms often created specialized roles among their top management group prior to going public in an effort to flesh out and highlight specialized expertise that would be favorably received by investors.

[54] See, for example, Stinchcombe, A. 1965. "Social Structures and Organization." In *Handbook of Organizations*, ed. J. March, 142–93. Chicago: Rand McNally.

[55] Porter, K., and W. Powell. 2006. "Networks and Organizations." In *The SAGE Handbook of Organization Studies*, eds. S. Clegg, C. Hardy, T. Lawrence and W. Nord, 779. 2nd ed. Thousand Oaks, CA: SAGE Publications (including citations to supporting studies of various researchers).

[56] Id.

[57] Id. at p. 780. For detailed discussion of social networks, see "Organizational Design: A Library of Resources for Sustainable Entrepreneurs" prepared and distributed by the Sustainable Entrepreneurship Project (www.seproject.org).

according to Reynolds and Miller, the startup process for launching a new business can begin with any of four key events—commitment, first financing, first hire, or first sale—and will be finished when and if each of those four events have been successfully completed. Among a group of more than 3,000 organizations surveyed by Reynolds and Moore, 85 percent of the respondents reported that commitment was the first event for them, an activity that included gathering information and resources and identifying potential customers and suppliers.[58] Researchers have also found that among high growth firms that successfully completed an initial public offering (IPO), those with extensive social resources, as measured by the company's business networks, personal networks, and number of underwriters subscribed to the IPO, were more successful in accumulating financial capital in the years leading up to their IPO than those firms that had fewer social resources.[59] In addition, studies have provided support for the proposition that science-based startups in the biotechnology sector have benefitted from early access to support and resources available from a diverse portfolio of highly central organizations.[60]

The primary reason that entrepreneurs contact others during the launch stage for their new businesses is to gain support and test their business ideas. In most cases, entrepreneurs will turn first to their family and friends for advice; however, there is evidence that during the launch stage the development and maintenance of social contacts, and where entrepreneurs invest the most time and effort in seeking advice and information, varies depending on the specific phase of organizational development. A study of how entrepreneurs in four countries developed their contacts found the same pattern in each country: entrepreneurs generally limited the size of their discussion networks when they were involved in developing the initial motivation necessary to support a decision to move forward

---

[58] Reynolds, P., and B. Miller. 1992. "New Firm Gestation: Conception, Birth, and Implications for Research." *Journal of Business Venturing* 7, no. 5, p. 405.

[59] Florin, J., M. Lubatkin, and W. Schulze. 2003. "A Social Capital Model of High-Growth Ventures." *Academy of Management Journal* 46, no. 3, p. 374.

[60] Powell, W., D. White, K. Koput, and J. Owen-Smith. 2005. "Network Dynamics and Field Evolution: The Growth of Inter-Organizational Collaboration in the Life Sciences." *American Journal of Sociology* 110, no. 4, pp. 1132–1205.

with launching a new venture; the size of their networks, and the time spent attempting to connect with others, expanded during the planning stage for the new venture; and the size of the network contracted, as did the time spent on working the network, as the entrepreneurs shifted their attention and energies toward actually establishing the new venture.[61]

While informal networks are important to entrepreneurs during the launch stage, it is clear that many entrepreneurs also seek advice, information, and other support from more formal role models, particularly potential sources of financial capital. Much attention has been paid to the role of "angel investors" who have been cited as being not only sources of seed capital but also as mentors who have been through the launch process and can provide entrepreneurs with access to a larger pool of potential resource providers and advice on how to be more effective in their entrepreneurial actions. In fact, one survey of angel investors in the United States found that more than half of them had provided one or more types of nonfinancial support to the entrepreneurs they had backed including involvement in creating or reshaping the business concept, helping recruit additional managers or members of the management team, and finding additional sources of financial capital. Only one in five of the angel investors helped their entrepreneurs with expanding their networks of personal and/or professional advisors or identifying prospective customers or suppliers.[62] Some studies of venture capitalists suggest that they play a similar role in "professionalizing" new ventures; however, rather than mentoring founders who may have more technical than managerial experience venture capitalists "contribute" by pushing to bring in outsiders to fill in an experienced management team.[63] Attorneys specializing in providing legal guidance to startups have been another source of formal mentoring

---

[61] Porter, K., and W. Powell. 2006. "Networks and Organizations." In *The SAGE Handbook of Organization Studies*, eds. S. Clegg, C. Hardy, T. Lawrence and W. Nord, 780. 2nd ed. Thousand Oaks, CA: SAGE Publications (citing Greve and Salaff 2003).

[62] Id. at p. 781 (citing Ardichvili et al 2000).

[63] Hellman, T., and M. Puri. 2002. "On the Fundamental Role of Venture Capital." *Federal Reserve Bank of Atlanta Economic Review, Fourth Quarter* 87, no. 4, pp. 19–24.

for entrepreneurs and have been able to provide them with information on the most effective path to forming and organizing a new company.

Founders/Owners Versus Professional Managers

The fundamental assumptions of the founder create the foundation for the distinctive characteristics or biases of the organizational culture of the company that tend to persist for as long as the company is run by the founder and/or his or her family members. These biases are highly valued by the first generation employees of the business since they are associated with the early success and ongoing survival of the company. All of this means that the founder's assumptions make an enduring mark on the company's organizational culture; however, growth, change, and the passage of time inevitably lead to challenges to those assumptions from other family members and nonfamily managers. In addition, the original assumptions may be called into question as new threats and opportunities arise in the company's "environment" that require new responses from the company in order for it to survive and prosper.

While it is certainly possible for the founder to remain in control of the management of the company for an extended period of time, and perhaps fill key management positions with other members of his or her family, more often than not the time comes when professional managers begin to fill key positions at various levels of the organizational structure. Schein observed that these professional managers are generally identified as nonfamily members and nonowners and it is assumed that they are less "invested" in the company than the founder and his or her family members.[64] Professional managers bring education and training that is specifically focused on management practices and techniques and this leads to skepticism regarding their level of commitment to retaining the original values and assumptions instilled by the founder during the early stages of the venture. While there is no doubt that professional managers can, and do, bring important organizational and functional skills to

---

[64] Schein, E. 1983. "The Role of the Founder in Creating Organizational Culture." In *Organizational Dynamics*, 348–64, 360. New York, NY: American Management Association.

the business long-time employees often fear that these managers are only concerned about short-term financial performance and not the founding assumptions.

Schein commented that while there are "strong stereotypic components" in the above-described differences between founder/owners and professional managers, there do appear to be clearly discernable differences between the two groups based on personality characteristics and the position that founders/owners occupy in the governance structure of their businesses. Schein went on to illustrate these differences by suggesting "stereotypes" for founders/owners and professional managers based on four dimensions: motivational/emotional, analytical, interpersonal, and structural/positional.[65]

First of all, Schein suggested that founders/owners are oriented toward creating and building; achievement-oriented; self-oriented and worried about their own image; have a high need for "glory"; jealous of their own prerogatives with a high need for autonomy; loyal to their own company; and willing and able to take moderate risks on their own authority. On the other hand, professional managers are oriented toward consolidating, surviving, and growing; power-and influence-oriented; organization-oriented and worried about the image of the company; interested in developing the organization and subordinates; loyal to the management profession and able to take risks albeit with more caution; and need for support. Schein also suggested that founders/owners could be described as "local" while professional managers tended to be "cosmopolitan."

Second, Schein believed that founders/owners are primarily intuitive, trusting of their own intuitions, and tend to have a long-range time horizon and are more holistic, meaning that they were better able to see the total picture and patterns. In contrast, professional managers are seen as primarily analytical and more cautious about relying on intuition, and tend to have a short-range time horizon, and are more specific in their worldview with greater focus on details and their consequences. Schein noted that the founders/owners are more likely than professional managers to be willing to try new, and risky, innovations based on little more

---

[65] Id. at p. 361.

than intuition while managers would rarely pursue such projects without first going through an extensive formal process of documentation, justification, and planning.[66]

Third, Schein described founders/owners as "particularistic," in the sense of seeing individuals as individuals; personal, political, and "involved"; centralist and autocratic; and emotional, impatient, and easily bored. In contrast, professional managers were described as "universalistic," meaning that they saw individuals as members of larger categories or groups such as employees, customers, or suppliers; impersonal, rational, and "uninvolved"; participative and delegation-oriented; and unemotional, patient, and persistent. Not surprisingly, Schein observed that while family ties were very important for founders/owners they were irrelevant for professional managers.

Finally, Schein suggested that there are a number of significant and interesting structural and positional differences between founders/owners and professional managers. With respect to founders/owners, he observed that they have the privileges and risks of "ownership" and have a secure managerial position because of their ownership stake; are generally highly visible and get close attention; have the support of family members involved in the business, an advantage that is tempered by the corresponding need to deal with family members and decide on the priorities between family and company issues; and have "weak bosses" since their ownership position allows them to install directors who are passive and subject to control by the founder/owner. On the other hand, professional managers generally have a minimal ownership stake in the business and thus have fewer ownership privileges and risks; have a less secure position because of their small ownership interest and thus must constantly prove themselves; are often invisible and do not get much attention; go about their business without the support of family members, which also means they do not have to worry about the distractions that might arise from potential conflicts between company and family issues; and have "strong bosses" on a board of directors that is independent and not controlled by the manager. It should be noted, however, that the lack of family support

---

[66] Id. at p. 362.

does not mean that professional managers cannot and do not have their own nonfamily support group within the organization. In addition, whether or not directors of large public corporations are truly independent of the chief executive officer has been a point of content since the CEO has often been given substantial latitude in selecting directors, thus resulting a board that may be reluctant to challenge the decisions of the CEO.

Schein also observed that founders fulfill several other unique functions during the early stages of development of the organizations that they create. For example, because of their ownership position and high level of personal confidence, founders are better situated than professional managers to contain and absorb the anxiety and risk that are often associated with new venture creation and are uniquely situated to assure others in the organization about the survival of the firm in what appear to be troubled times. In addition, because they are the primary stakeholders of the firm founders can pursue strategies that may not be optimal from a strictly financial perspective yet are seen as necessary to embed the values and biases of the founder and achieve the personal objectives of the founder for the business. Illustrations of this include insisting on broad participation in decision making even if this slows the process, avoiding layoffs during periods when operational performance is lagging, or insisting that family members perform roles within the company for which they are only marginally qualified.

Schein concluded that as the company grows and matures and professional managers begin to play a more significant role in the way the firm is operated and decisions are made it is inevitable that changes in the organizational culture will occur. Specifically, what Schein characterized as the "community feeling" instilled by the founder/owner is eventually overcome by the features of a more rational and bureaucratic organization imposed by the professional managers who are not invested in the original assumptions and values and who are not able to fulfill the unique functions of the founders/owners described above. How much of the original assumptions and values will survive the transition to professional management, and in what form, is generally somewhat of a mystery; however, to some extent the answer depends on the personal growth and evolution of the first- and second-generation employees and how they integrate the assumptions and values with the lessons they learn on their own as they become more experienced managers. Schein referred to this process as "hybridization" and suggested that an enlightened founder/owner would recognize and accept that there are new assumptions that lead to better solutions for the new external and internal problems confronting the company and will permit these assumption to become part of the organizational culture of the firm, a culture that would, in Schein's words, "maintain key old assumptions yet add relevant new ones." Schein suggested that the success and ease of the transition through the hybridization process depends on the ability and willingness of the founder/owner to facilitate the transition and accept succession to the next generation without perceiving it as a political or power struggle. Many students of new venture creation and growth have observed that succession planning is one of the most difficult and emotional challenges for such ventures.

Founders or Professional Managers?: The Israeli Experience

The influence of venture capitalists from the United States and Europe on their Israeli portfolio companies is often seen when decisions are being made regarding the role of the Israeli founders and whether or not a professional manager should be brought in to take on CEO responsibilities. Many of the issues that must be considered are not that different than those that arise when the investors and founders are all from one country, such as the United States; however, cultural differences must be taken into account when, for example, U.S. venture capitalists are insisting on bringing in experienced professional managers to oversee all of the operations of an Israeli firm (i.e., a CEO) and/or an important function (e.g., a CFO to make sure that "costs are being controlled"). Tolkowsky, who has studied the experiences of a number of Israeli technology startups, reported that attempts by U.S. venture capitalists to appoint a U.S. CEO without placing one of the Israeli founders on a "shoulder-to-shoulder" basis with the U.S. appointee (even if reporting to the CEO) had generally not been successful. Another attempt by U.S. investors to impose on the management structure of an Israeli company was demanding that the company recruit a U.S.-based CFO and this also was counterproductive since it deprived the CEO, who was Israeli, with close and easy access to a senior management team member with whom the CEO needed to have a trusting and intimate relationship.

Source: Tolkowsky, G. August 17, 2009. "Globalization of Technology Ventures: Lessons from Israel," Knowledge@Wharton.

CHAPTER 7

Founder's Role with IPO Firms

Introduction

There are probably numerous factors that motivate founders to form a new enterprise and invest the substantial amount of time and resources necessary to try and make the enterprise successful. Money, an opportunity for personal wealth maximization, is obviously important; however, founders often take the plunge because of their personal drive and ambition to carry out their "vision" and create and lead an organization dedicated to fulfilling that vision. The founder's vision is certainly important during the early stages of the venture. As Wasserman explains:

> At the start, the enterprise is only an idea in the mind of its founder, who possesses all the insights about the opportunity; about the innovative product, service, or business model that will capitalize on that opportunity; and about who the potential customers are. The founder hires people to build the business according to that vision and develops close relationships with those first employees. The founder creates the organizational culture, which is an extension of his or her style, personality and preferences.[1]

All these things are essential for survival but the problem is that founders often become so attached to the whole thing and overconfident about how essential they are to the firm that they may have difficulties understanding how their roles may need to change as the business matures.

---

[1] Wasserman, N. February 2008. "The Founder's Dilemma." *Harvard Business Review* 86, no. 2, pp. 103–09, 104.

The issue of the evolving role of the founder is especially important for companies that are on a path toward an initial public offering (IPO).

Founders may bring a variety of management styles and skills to their service as a chief executive officer (CEO) of their firm. At the startup stage, for example, operational skills are particularly important and emphasis is placed on the ability to manage the startup process, understand industry trends and requirements, and gain knowledge of the "cutting edge" technology that the firm must develop or otherwise acquire in order to find a competitive niche. As the firm evolves and matures, however, the relative importance of operational versus strategic skills begins to change and investors, such as venture capitalists, and other market observers focus on the strategic leadership skills of the CEO that are perceived to be essential for a successful transition of the firm from private to public company status.[2]

Certainly there are many founders who are committed to achieving the market recognition and financial achievement associated with an IPO for their firm. Jain and Tabak aptly described an IPO as "a major accomplishment for the founder(s) and a testament to their founding vision, creativity, strategic direction and management skills."[3] However, among the critical decisions that must be made in anticipation of an IPO is who should lead the firm as it makes the transition from private to public company status. Proponents of the "life cycle" theory of the firm argue that the evolution and growth of an entrepreneurial firm calls for changes in the managerial styles and capabilities of the CEO and other members of the senior management team since the primary focus of the leadership is shifting from viability and survival to management of complex organizational systems.[4] For example, it has been claimed that a CEO of a public

---

[2] Jain, B., and F. Tabak. 2008. "Factors Influencing the Choice Between Founder Versus Non-Founder CEOs for IPO Firms." *Journal of Business Venturing* 23, no. 1, pp. 21–45, 28.

[3] Id. at p. 21.

[4] Greiner, L. 1972. "Evolution and Revolution as Organizations Grow." *Harvard Business Review* 50, pp. 37–46; Boeker, W., and R. Karichalil. 2002. "Entrepreneurial Transitions: Factors Influencing Founder Departure." *Academy of Management Journal* 45, no. 3, pp. 818–26; Rubenson, G., and A. Gupta. 1992. "Replacing the Founder: Exploding the Myth of the Entrepreneur's Disease."

company must have specific skills, knowledge, experience, and social networks that are significantly different from those that a CEO must have when the firm is first launched and commentators have emphasized that the CEO of an IPO firm must be prepared to deal with a wide array of new and unique challenges, including changes in the corporate governance model, a significant increase in outside investor participation and scrutiny, increased market monitoring, and the potential for unexpected and unwanted attempts to seize corporate control and continuous pressure to meet expectations of market observers (e.g., analysts).[5]

While the IPO is certainly a milestone that triggers debate about whether or not a founder CEO should remain in the position, Wasserman argues that the crisis actually occurs much earlier when the company has completed its first major activity, such as the completion of development of its initial product or service and the subsequent launch of the product or service into the marketplace. While founders often believe, not unreasonably, that venture capitalists and other investors will see the release of the initial product or service and receipt of the revenues from that product or service as a validation of their leadership skills, the reality is that outsiders now look at the firm differently and see new challenges that require different management skills that the founder may not have in his or her toolbox. Some of the challenges that Wasserman cataloged for firms after they ship their initial product included building the capacity for marketing, manufacturing, and selling large volumes of product and providing the necessary post-sale support to a growing number of customers; implementing systems and procedures to address more complex finance and accounting issues, including selecting and overseeing finance executives and accountants; and creating and managing a more hierarchical

Business Horizons 35, no. 6, pp. 53–57; and Tushman, M., and E. Romanelli. 1985. "Organizational Evolution: A Metamorphosis Model of Convergence and Reorientation." In *Research in Organizational Behavior*, eds. L. Cummings and B. Straw, 171–222. Greenwich, CT: JAI Press.

[5] Jain, B., and F. Tabak. 2008. "Factors Influencing the Choice Between Founder Versus Non-Founder CEOs for IPO firms." *Journal of Business Venturing* 23, no. 1, pp. 21–45, 23.

organizational structure, including increased reliance of formal rules and processes and functional specialists.[6]

There are certainly examples of well-known and successful companies that have gone public with one of their founders as CEO and, in fact, researchers have presented evidence that one-third to one-half of IPO firms have gone public with founders as CEO and have actually had higher IPO valuations than companies that have gone public with nonfounder CEOs[7]; however, a large percentage of IPO companies have replaced their founder CEO with an outside professional deemed to be more qualified for the task of "going public." In some cases the founder may not be prepared or able to develop the skills necessary to lead a public company and this is certainly not a criticism of the founder since it is certainly difficult for anyone to have all the tools required to bring a firm through all of the challenges that must be addressed from the very beginning to the point where it has matured into an IPO candidate.[8] An alternative explanation, however, is that other factors trigger a change in the leadership of the firm as the IPO approaches including the desire of venture capitalists and other outside investors to send a signal to the market (i.e., investment bankers, institutional/retail investors, and analysts) regarding the proposed strategic direction and growth strategies of the company once the IPO has been completed. This follows from the assumption, as suggested by various researchers, that there are significant differences between the decision-making behavior, strategic choices, and performance of founder and nonfounder CEOs,[9] and that a firm's choice

---

[6] Wasserman, N. February 2008. "The Founder's Dilemma." *Harvard Business Review* 86, no. 2, pp. 103–09, 106.

[7] Certo, S., J. Covin, C. Daily, and D. Dalton. 2001. "Wealth and Effects of Founder Management Among IPO Stage New Ventures." *Strategic Management Journal* 22, nos. 6–7, pp. 641–58; and Nelson, T. 2003. "The Persistence of Founder Influence: Management, Ownership, and Performance Effects at Initial Public Offering." *Strategic Management Journal* 24, no. 8, pp. 707–24.

[8] Stevenson, H., and J. Jarillo. 1990. "A Paradigm of Entrepreneurship: Entrepreneurship Management." *Strategic Management Journal* 11, pp. 17–27.

[9] Jayaraman, N., A. Khorana, E. Nelling, and J. Covin. 2000. "CEO Founder Status and Firm Financial Performance." *Strategic Management Journal* 21, no. 12, pp. 1215–24; and Nelson, T. 2003. "The Persistence of Founder Influence:

between a founder and nonfounder leader thus provides the market with valuable information regarding strategic direction, growth strategy and investment, and financial policies that the market can use to predict post-IPO performance and place a value on the firm at the time of the IPO.

Wasserman suggests that founders themselves can reduce the stress and drama associated with succession issues by asking themselves hard questions about their own motivations, particularly whether motivated more by wealth than control or vice-versa. According to Wasserman, founders who are primarily motivated by control can be expected to proceed more slowly and cautiously in allowing outsiders to become involved with the company as cofounders, investors, or employees and will seek to guard their ability to maintain control at each stage of the process of developing new products and services, expanding human resources, and tapping into outside capital. On the other hand, wealth-motivated founders are more open to any reasonable strategy for increasing the value of their ownership stake in the company and thus are more likely to aggressively pursue venture capital even at the risk of losing control of the board of directors and support bringing on an experienced nonfounder CEO who can accelerate the growth of the company even if that means that the founder's equity stake is diluted.[10] Founders should be mindful of the fact that venture capitalists often will not invest in founder-led companies unless and until they have a good idea of the founder's motivations. In some cases, venture capitalists will not look at a firm unless the founder is driven to make money from the business. In other situations, venture capitalists not only want founders who seek financial success but also want to be comfortable that the founders have the leadership and management skills to provide long-term leadership for the firm that extends beyond startup and release of the first product or service.[11]

Management, Ownership, and Performance Effects at Initial Public Offering." *Strategic Management Journal* 24, no. 8, pp. 707–24.

[10] Wasserman, N. 2013. *The Founder's Dilemmas: Anticipating and Avoiding the Pitfalls That Can Sink a Startup.* Princeton, NJ: Princeton University Press.

[11] Wasserman, N. February 2008. "The Founder's Dilemma." *Harvard Business Review*, no. 2, pp. 103–09, 107–08.

One of the most important studies of how an IPO influences CEO succession among emerging companies was undertaken by Jain and Tabak, who used a database that included 231 firms that completed IPOs in 1997 and which had raised, on average, $45 million in the IPO and enjoyed first-day increases from their offering price averaging a little over 17 percent.[12] Jain and Tabak examined a host of factors discussed below that they hypothesized might influence the choice of founder versus non-founder CEOs for IPO firms and concluded that

> output-based founder functional background, size of founding team, and insider presence on the board raise the probability of founder CEO at IPO while founder age, VC influence on board, TMT independence, and outside blockholder ownership lower the probability of founder CEO at IPO.[13]

Jain and Tabak also observed industry variations in the proportion of firms with founder CEOs at IPO.[14] For example, the probability of a founder CEO at the time of the IPO was higher in high-technology industries.[15] Industry variations in the proportion of CEOs with output functional backgrounds were also observed.[16]

A similar study by Wasserman of 212 startup companies in the United States formed during the late 1990s and early 2000s also provided support for the relatively early departure of founders from control over the management of the firms: 50 percent of the founders in the study group were no longer CEO after three years, 60 percent of the founders

---

[12] Jain, B., and F. Tabak. 2008. "Factors Influencing the Choice Between Founder Versus Non-Founder CEOs for IPO Firms." *Journal of Business Venturing* 23, no. 1, pp. 21–45, 24 (citing Wasserman, N. 2003. "Founder-CEO Succession and the Paradox of Entrepreneurial Success." *Organization Science* 14, no. 2, pp. 149–72).

[13] Jain, B., and F. Tabak. 2008. "Factors Influencing the Choice Between Founder Versus Non-Founder CEOs for IPO firms." *Journal of Business Venturing* 23, no. 2, pp. 21–45, 41.

[14] Id. at p. 35.

[15] Id. at p. 40.

[16] Id. at p. 36.

were no longer CEO after four years and more than 75 percent of the founders had left the CEO position by the time their firms completed an IPO.[17] Interestingly, four out of five of the founders in Wasserman's study who had left the CEO position did so against their will and Wasserman correctly observed that "[t]he change in leadership can be particularly damaging when employees loyal to the founder oppose it" and "the manner in which founders tackle their first leadership transition often makes or breaks young enterprises."[18] Wasserman acknowledged that the IPO was certainly an important and well-recognized milestone for high growth companies; however, he pointed out that research conducted on early stage Internet firms found evidence that founder CEO succession was often triggered by other significant corporate milestone events such as completion of product development and/or raising capital from outside investors.[19]

Factors Influencing Founder Leadership at IPO

As noted above, Jain and Tabak examined a host of factors that they hypothesized might be significantly related to the probability of ongoing founder leadership as the CEO at the time of IPO, including founder characteristics such as functional background and age, the size of the founding team, board composition, top management team independence, outside blockholder ownership, the company's demand for equity financing, and the extent of involvement and influence of venture capitalists.[20] In selecting the factors for analysis Jain and Tabak noted that in the context of "signaling theory" the choice between a founder and a nonfounder to lead the firm through the IPO and into public company status would likely be viewed by market participants as an informative

---

[17] Wasserman, N. February 2008. "The Founder's Dilemma." *Harvard Business Review* 86, no. 2, pp. 103–09, 104.

[18] Id.

[19] Wasserman, N. 2003. "Founder-CEO Succession and the Paradox of Entrepreneurial Success." *Organization Science* 14, no. 2, pp. 149–72.

[20] Jain, B., and F. Tabak. 2008. "Factors Influencing the Choice Between Founder Versus Non-Founder CEOs for IPO Firms." *Journal of Business Venturing* 23, no. 1, pp. 21–45, 41.

signal regarding the firm's strategic direction and growth strategies.[21] Jain and Tabak also referenced the "sociological perspective" as support for the proposition that IPO firms would likely select the CEO at the time of their IPO based on the characteristics that they believed would be most appealing to investor groups, which the firms hoped would be the most important in stimulating demand for their stock and increasing the overall valuation of the firm.[22]

These theories provided the basis for a number of hypotheses which were empirically tested by Jain and Tabak. For example, they suggested that it was reasonable to assume that the functional background of the CEO at the time of the IPO would be a potentially informative signal to the marketplace of the firm's intentions with regard to growth strategy, investment decisions, and financial policies and that investors would have higher expectations of the firm's intent and ability to aggressively invest in research and development, new product development, and acquisitions if the CEO of the newly public company had demonstrable experience in output-based functions. Accordingly, they constructed and tested a hypothesis, as described below, that the probability of a founder CEO at IPO was higher for founders with career experiences in output-based functions. Other hypotheses incorporated additional elements into a complex picture such as the influence of venture capital participation and, in fact, Jain and Tabak hypothesized that involvement of venture capitalists in the governance of an IPO candidate moderated the relationship between the founder's functional background and the probability that the founder would still be the CEO at the time of the IPO.

Founder's Career Experience and Functional Background

It is no surprise that persons who rise to the top levels of management come from a variety of functional backgrounds and the experience and training they receive in their functional areas influence the perspective they

---

[21] Id. at pp. 24–25.

[22] For more on the "sociological perspective," see Davis, G. 2005. "New Directions in Corporate Governance." *Annual Review of Sociology* 31, pp. 143–62.

bring to discharging their duties as a senior executive and, in particular, the strategic decisions that they make regarding the overall direction of their firms.[23] This is so even though a CEO is presumed to have a more "generalist" perspective and is expected to act in a manner that is not overly influenced by the requirements or requests of any single functional department.

Several models have been suggested for classifying various functional paths and assigning projected characteristics to executives that follow those paths. For example, researchers have distinguished between "output" functions, such as marketing/sales and product development, and "throughput" functions, such as production, accounting, finance, and process engineering.[24] They have gone on to suggest that executives with a foundation in output functions are more likely to focus on "organizational innovation and growth" since those functions are more involved with growth-oriented activities such as generation of new ideas, opportunities, products, and services. On the other hand, executives coming from one of the throughput functions are expected to be stronger candidates for providing internal and external stability. Another model suggests that the learning experiences and decision-making focus of managers differ depending on whether their development occurred in "upstream" or "downstream" companies.[25] Managers from upstream companies, where decision making is more focused on raw materials and production, have a stronger grounding in standardization and efficiency techniques and thus tend to focus their actions and decisions on process development and capital expenditures. However, managers from downstream companies, where decision making is more focused on sales, are steeped in the advantages of customization and innovation and, not surprisingly, are more

[23] See, for example, Astley, W., R. Axelsson, R. Butler, D. Hickson, and D. Wilson. 1982. "Complexity and Cleavage: Dual Explanations of Strategic Decision-Making." *Journal of Management Studies* 19, no. 4, pp. 357–75.

[24] Hambrick, D., and P. Mason. 1984. "Upper Echelons: The Organization as a Reflection of its Top Managements." *Academy of Management Review* 9, no. 2, pp. 193–206.

[25] Galbraith, J. 1983. "Strategy and Organization Planning." *Human Resource Management* 22, nos. 1–2, pp. 63–77.

likely to focus their strategic decisions on research and development, product development, and marketing.

The career experience and functional background of founders have often been cited as significant considerations for venture capitalists deciding whether to invest in a particular company and the consensus is that venture capitalists consider these factors to be important in measuring the prospects for success of their portfolio companies.[26] Jain and Tabak suggested that the probability of a founder CEO at IPO would be higher when market participants believed that the founder's experience and functional background had adequately provided him or her with the knowledge, skills, and vision thought to be necessary for effectively overseeing the transition of the firm to public company status. They tested the hypothesis that "[t]he probability of founder CEO at IPO is higher for founders with career experiences in output-based functions" and found that founders with output-based functional backgrounds were indeed significantly more likely to assume the CEO position at IPO compared to founders with throughput-based functional backgrounds.[27] Jain and Tabak also found that prior experience in "downstream" businesses increased the likelihood of founder CEOs for IPO firms.[28]

Specific findings of Jain and Tabak indicated that founders with career experience in product research and development were more likely to retain the CEO position at IPO relative to founders with experience in other functional tracks.[29] Jain and Tabak observed that their findings were consistent with evidence from other studies that highlighted the

---

[26] Jain, B., and F. Tabak. 2008. "Factors Influencing the Choice Between Founder Versus Non-Founder CEOs for IPO Firms." *Journal of Business Venturing* 23, no. 1, pp. 21–45, 26 (citing MacMillan, I., R. Siegel, and P. SubbaNarasimhan. 1985. "Criteria Used by Venture Capitalists to Evaluate New Business Proposals." *Journal of Business Venturing* 1, pp. 119–28; and Riquelme, H., and T. Richard. 1992. "Hybrid Conjoint Analysis: An Estimation Probe in New Venture Directions." *Journal of Business Venturing* 7, no. 6, pp. 505–18).

[27] Jain, B., and F. Tabak. 2008. "Factors Influencing the Choice Between Founder Versus Non-Founder CEOs for IPO Firms." *Journal of Business Venturing* 23, no. 1, pp. 21–45, 26.

[28] Id. at pp. 40–42.

[29] Id. at p. 22.

value and potential benefits of a background in R&D for top managers of high-technology businesses. For example, other researchers have argued that executives with R&D backgrounds are perceived as representing progress and invention, better able to react to changes in product design and technologies, and more likely to pursue investments in R&D.[30] In addition, researchers and investors have frequently suggested that senior managers with an R&D background are critically important in technology-based industries where technical expertise and development of innovative products is necessary in order to carve out a sustainable competitive advantage.[31] Jain and Tabak noted that while functional experience was important, the ideal type of CEO at IPO was someone who also had the strategic vision, experience, and credibility to manage and complete the difficult IPO process.[32]

Founder's Age

According to Jain and Tabak various researchers had argued that, in comparison to their younger colleagues, older managers were more risk averse, less likely to invest in growth strategies, and had greater difficulties in learning new behaviors and understanding new ideas.[33] If this

---

[30] Id. at p. 41 (citing Barker, V., and G. Mueller. 1995. "CEO Characteristics and Firm R&D Spending." *Management Science* 48, no. 6, pp. 782–801; Waller, M., G. Huber, and W. Glick. 1995. "Functional Background as a Determinant of Executive's Selection Perception." *Academy of Management Journal* 38, no. 4, pp. 943–74).

[31] Id. (citing Hambrick, D. 1981. "Environment, Strategy, and Power Within Top Management Teams." *Administrative Science Quarterly*, pp. 253–76); Hambrick, D., C. Black, and J. Fredrickson. 1992. "Executive Leadership of the High-Technology Firm: What Is Special About It?" In *Advances in Global High-technology Management*, eds. L. Gomez-Mejia and M. Lawless, 3–18. Greenwich, CT: JAI Press.

[32] Jain. B., and F. Tabak. 2008. "Factors Influencing the Choice Between Founder Versus Non-Founder CEOs for IPO firms." *Journal of Business Venturing* 23, no. 1, pp. 21–45, 28.

[33] Id. at p. 26 (citing Bantel, K., and S. Jackson. 1989. "Top Management Innovations in Banking: does the Demography of the Top Team Make a Difference?" *Strategic Management Journal* 10, nos. S1, pp. 107–24; Barker, V., and

characterization of older managers was accurate it could be expected that
the probability of a founder CEO at IPO would be negatively related to
the age of the founder since the suggested "conservative and risk-averse
strategic orientation" of an older CEO would adversely impact the performance of the firm in an environment where competitiveness turned on
being willing and eager to pursue growth through high-risk investments
that required large expenditures on research and development and capital
equipment.[34] Jain and Tabak did find that there was a negative relationship between founder age and probability of a founder CEO at IPO and
explained that "[s]ince age is a proxy for risk and effort aversion, our
results suggest that IPO investors seek low risk and effort aversion from
CEO candidates."[35]

Size of the Founding Team

Jain and Tabak found a positive relationship between the size of the founding team and the probability of a founder CEO at IPO. The researchers
commented that "[o]ur results are . . . consistent with the notion that
larger founding teams increase the bargaining power of founder CEOs as
well as provide firms with a deeper bench of individuals who can assume
the CEO position at IPO."[36] They had noted that other researchers had
suggested that a founder leader of a large founding team would be more
likely to be able to retain his or her position for a longer period of time,
particularly when the other founders provided complimentary skills and

---

G. Mueller. 2002. "CEO Characteristics and Firm R&D Spending." *Management
Science* 48, no. 6, pp. 782–801; Child, J. 1974. "Managerial and Organizational
Factors Associated with Company Performance." *Journal of Management Studies*
11, no. 3, pp. 13–27; and Hambrick, D., and P. Mason. 1984. "Upper Echelons:
The Organization as a Reflection of its Top Managements." *Academy of Manage-
ment Review* 9, no. 2, pp. 193–206).

[34] Jain, B., and F. Tabak. 2008. "Factors Influencing the Choice Between
Founder Versus Non-Founder CEOs for IPO firms." *Journal of Business Venturing*
23, no. 1, pp. 21–45, 26.

[35] Id. at p. 22.

[36] Id.

experiences.[37] Jain and Tabak also suggested that the other founders on a large founding team could effectively monitor the actions of a CEO chosen from among them, thereby alleviating concerns that outside investors might have that the founder CEO would make nonvalue-maximizing decisions.

Board Composition

Researchers have argued that board composition, particularly the degree of "independence" among the directors, will have a significant influence on whether or not a founder CEO is retained at the time of an IPO. While there are benefits to insider representation on the board, including their direct knowledge of firm operational activities and continuous daily exposure to the firm's competitive and technological environment, it is suspected that insiders, often handpicked by founder CEOs, may be more reluctant that outsiders to cast aside a founder CEO in favor of a nonfounder replacement at the time of an IPO.[38] The aversion to change may be even greater in situations where the insiders do not have a large amount of "skin in the game" in the form of ownership interests in the firm. Accordingly Jain and Tabak hypothesized, and their results confirmed, that the probability of a founder CEO at IPO is positively related to the proportion of insiders on the board of directors.[39] In turn, the probability of a founder CEO at IPO decreases with board independence, either as a result of larger outside director presence or higher top management team ownership, or a combination of the two.[40] Jain and

---

[37] Id. at p. 27 (citing Wasserman, N. 2003. "Founder-CEO Succession and the Paradox of Entrepreneurial Success." *Organization Science* 14, no. 2, pp. 149–72).

[38] Fiet, J., L. Busenitz, D. Moesel, and J. Barney. 1997. "Complementary Theoretical Perspectives on the Dismissal of New Venture Team Members." *Journal of Business Venturing* 12, no. 5, pp. 347–66.

[39] Jain, B., and F. Tabak. 2008. "Factors Influencing the Choice Between Founder Versus Non-Founder CEOs for IPO Firms." *Journal of Business Venturing* 23, no. 1, pp. 21–45, 30, 42.

[40] Id.

Tabak also found that firms with a founder CEO at IPO tended to have smaller boards than firms with a nonfounder CEO at IPO.[41]

Top Management Team Independence

The CEO, founder or otherwise, and other members of the top management team (TMT) all derive power from their individual equity ownership of the firm and researchers have suggested that the chances of a founder CEO being deposed at IPO are positively related to the extent of the "independence" of other members of the TMT as measured by their percentage equity ownership of the firm.[42] In other words, when other top managers have accumulated their own significant equity stake in the firm they are less beholden to a particular founder CEO and are more likely to have interests that are aligned with outsiders holding large blocks of stock, such as venture capitalists. This means that these top managers would be more likely to facilitate removal of a founder CEO if they believed that recruiting a more qualified outsider would maximize the value of their shareholdings at and after an IPO. Jain and Tabak tested the hypothesis that "the probability of founder CEO at IPO is negatively related to the extent of TMT independence" and found support for the hypothesis.[43]

Outside Blockholder Ownership

Jain and Tabak tested the hypothesis that "the probability of founder CEO at IPO is negatively related to the extent of outside blockholder

---

[41] Id. at p. 37.

[42] Several researchers have suggested that one important determinant of the "power" of a CEO is the amount of equity held by other top managers of the firm. See, for example, Fredrickson, J., D. Hambrick, and S. Baumrin. 1988. "A Model of CEO Dismissal." *Academy of Management Review* 13, no. 2, pp. 255–70; and Rubenson, G., and A. Gupta. 1992. "Replacing the Founder: Exploding the Myth of the Entrepreneur's Disease." *Business Horizons* 35, no. 6, pp. 53–57.

[43] Jain, B., and F. Tabak. 2008. "Factors Influencing the Choice Between Founder Versus Non-Founder CEOs for IPO firms." *Journal of Business Venturing* 23, no. 1, pp. 21–45, 31.

ownership."[44] They observed that concentration of large blocks of shares in the hands of outside investors provided those investors with the power to influence decisions regarding the appointment of the CEO and other members of the top management team and regulate the power and influence of the top managers of the firm.[45] In the context of a pending IPO, outside blockholders can influence the strategic, operational, and personnel decisions that must be made by the firm, including the choice of the person who will lead the firm as CEO through the IPO process, and Jain and Tabak found that higher outside blockholder ownership lowered the probability of a founder CEO at IPO.

Demand for Equity Financing

Jain and Tabak noted that one of the main reasons that firms undertake an IPO and assume the duties and obligations associated with public company status is to gain access to the broader range of financing methods that are available in public equity and debt markets. Jain and Tabak pointed out that investors interested in participating in an IPO do so with the expectation that the company will aggressively pursue opportunities in the public capital markets after the IPO and use the proceeds to finance growth strategies that will ultimately create extraordinary value for the public shareholders. They suggested that while IPO issuing companies could access debt financing it was more likely that they would rely on equity financing since they were "usually smaller, less profitable, with stronger growth opportunities, and lower collateral value of assets relative to a typical seasoned firm."[46]

---

[44] Id.

[45] Id. (citing Wasserman, N. 2003. "Founder-CEO Succession and the Paradox of Entrepreneurial Success." *Organization Science* 14, no. 2, pp. 149–72); Boeker, W. 1992. "Power and Managerial Dismissal: Scapegoating at the Top." *Administrative Science Quarterly* 37, pp. 400–21; and Denis, D.J., D.K. Denis, and A. Sarin. 1997. "Ownership Structure and Top Executive Turnover." *Journal of Financial Economics* 45, no. 2, pp. 193–221.

[46] Id. (citing Eckbo, B., and Ø. Norli. 2005. "Liquidity Risk, Leverage, and Long-Run IPO Returns." *Journal of Corporate Finance* 11, nos. 1–2, pp. 1–35).

Jain and Tabak argued that founder CEOs, who typically have relatively large ownership stakes in their firms at the time of the IPO, might be wary of raising additional capital through equity financing after the IPO due to concerns about dilution of ownership and control. While this is certainly understandable from the individual perspective of the founder CEO, it has significant consequences for the success of the IPO since prospective investors might be put off if they see the choice to maintain a founder as CEO as a signal that the company would take a more conservative approach toward seeking equity financing after the IPO and that prospects for appreciation of shareholder value would be reduced accordingly. Jain and Tabak speculated that growth-oriented companies with a projected strong demand for equity capital would be more likely to go public with a nonfounder CEO less burdened by concerns relating to dilution and control; however, they found no support for the hypothesis that "the probability of founder CEO at IPO is negatively related to the demand for equity capital."[47]

Venture Capital Participation

Research indicates that the quality of the CEO is a significant factor for venture capitalists when they are deciding whether to invest in a particular firm and that when making that decision venture capitalists carefully analyze the capabilities, career experiences, and track record of the founder CEO in order to assess whether he or she is likely to be able to provide the leadership, strategic direction, and vision necessary for the firm to mature and successfully complete a transition to public company status. At the time that the investment decision is being made venture capitalists are particularly interested in whether or not the founder CEO is familiar with managing the startup process and in the founder's experience in the particular industry and the founder's knowledge of the relevant technology. The potential problem is that a founder CEO who is well suited to managing the startup may not be able to develop the management skills

---

[47] Jain, B., and F. Tabak. 2008. "Factors Influencing the Choice Between Founder Versus Non-Founder CEOs for IPO firms." *Journal of Business Venturing* 23, no. 1, pp. 21–45, 31.

perceived to be needed as the firm evolves to public company status. For example, researchers have argued that while managers do acquire new skills as time goes by it is often difficult for them to make fundamental changes in their management styles[48] and venture capitalists may fear that a founder CEO may be unable to provide the "strategic leadership skills" that become increasingly important, in relation to "operational skills," as firms grow and approached the threshold of public company status.

Jain and Tabak hypothesized that venture capital participation would be an important factor in whether or not a founder CEO retained his or her position at the time of the IPO and that venture capital participation likely reduced the probability of a founder CEO at IPO. They noted that "[d]ue to their industry and product market expertise, and the nature of their repeated and on-going involvement in the IPO market, VCs are in a unique position to identify skills sets and career experiences required of CEOs to successfully navigate a firm through its IPO."[49] As such, if venture capitalists were indeed concerned that a founder CEO did not have the desired strategic skills, it is reasonable to expect that venture capitalists would ultimately seek to replace the founder CEO with an outsider that brings experience, strategic vision, and credibility to the IPO process.[50]

---

[48] Barrick, M., and M. Mount. 1991. "The Big Five Personality Dimensions and Job Performance: A Meta Analysis." *Personal Psychology* 44, no. 1, pp. 1–26.

[49] Jain, B., and F. Tabak. 2008. "Factors Influencing the Choice Between Founder Versus Non-Founder CEOs for IPO Firms." *Journal of Business Venturing* 23, no. 1, pp. 21–45, 27.

[50] Id. at p. 28 (citing Fried, V., and R. Hisrich. 1995. "The Venture Capitalist: a Relationship Investor." *California Management Review* 37, no. 2, pp. 101–13; Bruton, G., V. Fried, and R. Hisrich. 1997. "Venture Capitalist and CEO Dismissal." *Entrepreneurship Theory and Practice* 21, no. 3, pp. 41–54; and Bruton, G., V. Fried, and R. Hisrich. 2000. "CEO Dismissal in Venture Capital-Backed Firms: Further Evidence From an Agency Perspective." *Entrepreneurship Theory and Practice* 24, no. 4, pp. 69–77). Research described in the cited articles indicates that a perceived lack of ability with regard to strategic leadership skills and disagreements regarding the future direction of the firm are more likely causes of replacement of a founder CEO by venture capitalists than managerial opportunism.

Interestingly, the presence or absence of venture capital involvement did not, in and of itself, have a significant impact on whether or not there was a founder CEO at IPO.[51] However, venture capital participation did lead to heightened focus on whether the founder CEO has the strategic vision, experience, and credibility to manage the IPO process. In addition, venture capitalists were more likely to accede to a founder CEO continuing at the helm of the firm when the founder has an output-based functional background, since the assumption was that his or her experience was well suited to creating and disseminating the required "growth story" required for IPO to be successful in the market.[52] Finally, the impact of venture capital participation was influenced by the size of their ownership stake, their proportionate representation on the board of directors, and covenants that might be included in the investment documentation. For example, if the venture capitalists have a strong position on the board of directors they are better positioned to influence the decisions that must be made regarding "going public" and exert pressure to make changes in the top management group, including the CEO position.[53] In fact, when venture capital investment was accompanied by a significant presence of their representatives of the venture capitalists on the board the probability of a founder CEO at IPO decreased.[54]

Methods for Keeping Founders on Board

Regardless of the reasons, the evidence is clear that a large percentage of founders will eventually leave the CEO position and this raises the issue of just how those founders can remained involved with the activities of their firm. The ideal solution was described by Wasserman: ". . . a board should keep the founder involved in some way, often as a board member, and use his or her relationships and knowledge to help the

---

[51] Id. at pp. 23 and 42.

[52] Id. at p. 28.

[53] Id. at p. 29 (citing Boeker, W., and R. Wiltbank. 2005. "New Venture Evolution and Managerial Capabilities." *Organization Science* 16, no. 2, pp. 123–33).

[54] Id. at p. 23.

new CEO succeed."[55] Unfortunately, many founders turn into negative influences with respect to their firm by resisting changes implemented by the new CEO and encouraging their followers to leave the company. In Wasserman's own study of succession among start-up firms 37 percent of the founders left their companies after a professional CEO was hired, 23 percent took a position below the new CEO, and 40 percent were assigned the role of "chairman."[56] Wasserman suggested that boards find ways to provide personal growth and fulfillment to founders in order to keep them happy and noted that some founders are provided with the resources to focus on their favorite functional area, such as engineering, or are provided with opportunities to learn new skills that will broaden their skill sets in anticipation of their next new venture.[57] Wasserman also commented that "the less similar the new CEO is to the founder—it the new CEO is 10 years older, for instance—the easier it is for the founder to accept the change."[58]

---

[55] Wasserman, N. February 2008. "The Founder's Dilemma." *Harvard Business Review* 86, no. 2, pp. 103–09. 108.

[56] Id.

[57] Id. Wasserman noted the experience of one founder who rotated through roles in a number of areas (e.g., finance, product marketing, and sales) after stepping down as CEO and who actually was given the opportunity to return as CEO down the road in light of the broader range of experience he had accumulated during the interim period.

[58] Id.

About the Author

Dr Alan S. Gutterman is the Founding Director of the Sustainable Entrepreneurship Project (www.seproject.org). In addition, Alan's prolific output of practical guidance and tools for legal and financial professionals, managers, entrepreneurs, and investors has made him one of the best-selling individual authors in the global legal publishing marketplace. His cornerstone work, *Business Transactions Solution*, is an online-only product available and featured on Thomson Reuter's Westlaw, the world's largest legal content platform, which includes almost 200 book-length modules covering the entire lifecycle of a business. Alan has also authored or edited over 40 books on sustainable entrepreneurship, management, business law and transactions, international law business and technology management for a number of publishers including Thomson Reuters, Kluwer, Aspatore, Oxford, Quorum, ABA Press, Aspen, Sweet & Maxwell, Euromoney, CCH, and BNA. Alan has over three decades of experience as a partner and senior counsel with internationally recognized law firms counselling small and large business enterprises in the areas of general corporate and securities matters, venture capital, mergers and acquisitions, international law and transactions, strategic business alliances, technology transfers, and intellectual property, and has also held senior management positions with several technology-based businesses including service as the chief legal officer of a leading international distributor of IT products headquartered in Silicon Valley and as the chief operating officer of an emerging broadband media company. He has been an adjunct faculty member at several colleges and universities, including Boalt Hall, Golden Gate University, Hastings College of Law, Santa Clara University, and the University of San Francisco, teaching classes on a diverse range of topics including corporate finance, venture capital, corporate law, Japanese business law, and law and economic development, He received his AB, MBA, and JD from the University of California at Berkeley, a DBA from Golden Gate University, and a PhD from the University of Cambridge. For more information about Alan, his publications, or the Sustainable Entrepreneurship Project, please contact him directly at alangutterman@gmail.com, and follow him on LinkedIn (https://linkedin.com/in/alangutterman/).

Index

www.ingramcontent.com/pod-product-compliance
Lightning Source LLC
Chambersburg PA
CBHW071848200326
41519CB00016B/4292

9 781948 976558